Artificial Intelligence for Beginners

Easy to Understand Guide of AI, Data Science, and Internet of Things. How to Use AI in Practice? Revelations of AI Superpowers Explained for the Real World

Jeff Mc Frockman

Table of Content

Introduction

Congratulations on downloading *Artificial Intelligence for Beginners: Easy to Understand Guide of AI, Data Science, and Internet of Things. How to Use AI in Practice? Revelations of AI Superpowers Explained for the Real World*, and thank you for doing so. With the constant increase in the generation of big data, we are forced to look for technologies that can help us make informed decisions. All professional fields have become very complex due to the growing demand to find the most efficient ways to extract value from the existing data. By downloading this book, you have taken the first step towards learning how to use big data and how artificial intelligence can make it possible to utilize the available data productively. The information that you find in the following chapters is very important as it will help you understand the role of artificial intelligence in society and its impact on your career.

To that end, this book provides an in-depth overview of artificial intelligence, highlighting its major concepts, its historical development, and application in various fields, including finance, business, and medicine, and the types of programming that are significant to artificial intelligence. It also covers the use of robotics and their role in the advancement of artificial intelligence, as well as how each influences the other. We have also comprehensively addressed the role of the Internet of Things (IoT) today. People can utilize so much from artificial intelligence and IoT to improve their lives and enhance their productivity. An interesting concept that we have also covered in the AI superpowers across the world, with a particular focus on China, which is the fastest rising region for AI development.

There are several books on Artificial Intelligence in the market, thanks again for choosing this one! I hope you enjoy reading!

Chapter 1: Artificial Intelligence Basic Terminologies

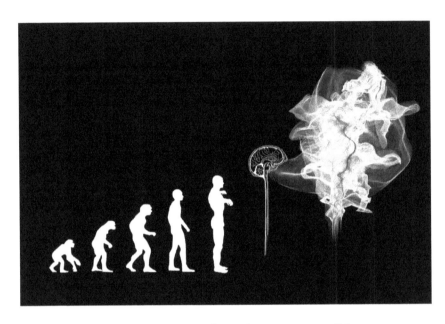

Artificial intelligence or simply AI is a term used in computer science to refer to the intelligence shown by machines as compared to the natural intelligence which human beings possess. The machines copy the human mind's functions and capabilities. The field of AI cut across key science areas such as human psychology, computer science, and cognitive science. There are key terms that are important if you are interested in learning Artificial intelligence. They include the following:

- **Abductive logic programming**

  This is one of the terms which you need to be familiar with. It refers to the area of AI that deals with the representation of information about the general world in a way that a computer system can make use in finding solutions for difficult tasks. The problems are arranged in an orderly manner to allow the computer to reach a conclusion based on a given premise.

- **AI-complete**

  In computer science, problems can be classified either as AI hard or AI-complete. An AI-complete or AI hard problem means that a problem can be as difficult as that of getting a solution to a key artificial intelligence. This then makes computers to be comparable to humans in terms of intelligence.

- **Approximate string matching**

  This is a method of locating strings that exactly match a given pattern. Approximate matching involves matching the strings by dividing it into two subproblems. You then locate the substring, which shares the same matches within the given string. String matching is an important cluster of string algorithms which are used to locate where one or more of strings are located inside a bigger text or string.

- **Algorithms**

  Algorithms basically refer to the set of rules or instructions which are given to an AI or other machines for the purpose of enabling it to learn on its own. Some of the key kinds of algorithms include classification, clustering, recommendation, and regression.

- **Artificial intelligence**

  This refers to the machine's ability to make significant decisions, which are similar to those made by the human mind. They use the same process as that used by the human mind in making decisions.

- **Artificial neural network (ANN)**

  ANN refers to a model that was designed to behave the same way as a human brain. It generates solutions to problems that prove challenging for normal computer systems to solve.

- **Automatic computing**

  This is a system's capability to manage its own resources in order to function optimally without your input.

- **Chatbots**

  A Chatbot is a chat robot that is made to carry out intelligent conversations with humans. Such conversations are carried out through text chats or voice commands. They make use of a computer interface with AI capabilities.

- **Classification**

  This type of algorithm enables the machines to give a type of specific data using the available training data.

- **Cluster analysis**

  This refers to the kind of unsupervised learning commonly designed for exploratory data analysis to locate missing patterns or groupings of data. They are created in the same way the metrics of Euclidean are.

- **Clustering**

  Clustering algorithms enable the machines to group data points into categories, which share the same characteristics.

- **Cognitive computing**

  This refers to the computerized model which copy the manner in which the human mind thinks. Cognitive computing happens when the machine is taken through a self-learning process through the use of data mining, pattern recognition, and NPL.

- **Convolutional neural network (CNN)**

  This refers to the kind of neural networks that locate and sensibly describes images.

- **Deep learning**

  This refers to the ability of an AI machine to mimic human thought patterns autonomously through neural networks that are made of cascading layers of data.

- **Decision tree**

  Decision tree refers to a decision model used to analyze decisions and the possible consequences of the decisions. The format of the decision tree is similar to a flow chart.

- **Game AI**

    This refers to a type of AI designed specifically for gaming. It makes use of an algorithm in order to replace randomness. Game AI is a digital behavior applied in non-player characters to give intelligence similar to those of humans and player actions taken by the player as a result of their reactions.

- **Genetic algorithm**

    This refers to an algorithm with similar principles guiding natural selection and genetics. It is used to come up with optimal solutions to challenging problems, which could take a long time to solve in normal circumstances.

- **Heuristic search methods**

    Refers to the system support, which reduces the search for solutions to a problem by getting rid of options which are not correct.

- **Knowledge Engineering**

    This is software engineering that generates general knowledge-based systems. The system is generally based and may have content touching on all areas such as technical, scientific, and social aspects.

- **Logic programming**

    Refers to programming type whereby you carry out computations drawn from the available knowledge section of facts and rules. Some of the examples of computer languages using logic programming are LISP and Prolog programming languages, which are widely used in AI programming.

- **Machine intelligence**

  This refers to the general concept, which includes machine learning, deep learning, and the learning of the general AI algorithms.

- **Machine learning**

  This refers to the type of AI which specializes in algorithms. In machine learning, the goal is to design machines that learn without the need for programming. The machines could also be altered when new data is exposed to it.

- **Machine perception**

  The capability of a machine for a system to get data from outside sources. The machine can then analyze and interpret the data in the same way that the human mind does. This is possible when both hardware and software data are attached.

- **Natural Language Processing.**

  This refers to the program which is designed in such a way that it can recognize and understand human communication.

- **Recurrent neural network (RNN)**

  This refers to the kind of designed program that makes sense of sequential information. The program then identifies patterns and create results based on the calculations of the given data.

- **Supervised learning**

  Refers to the learning in which output data sets are trained to give expected algorithms in the same manner in which a classroom teacher trains a student

- **Swarm behavior**

  This refers to the ability of a machine to follow the rules without involving central coordination.

- **Unsupervised learning**

  This refers to the machine learning algorithm, which is used to come up with inferences from datasets without labeled responses from the input data.

The Basic Concepts You Need to Be Aware in Artificial Intelligence

In order for you to understand the more profound concepts which are key in AI. you need to understand some basic terms of AI. These includes:

- **Machine Learning**

  Machine learning is a type of AI that enables machines to learn tasks without the preexisting code. Machines are given a large number of trial tasks. They are then allowed to go through the trials. The machines are then allowed to learn and adapt their own methods in order to achieve the given goals. For example, you can give a machine several images to analyze and recognize. The machine will go through several permutations in order to acquire the ability to correctly identify patterns or shapes in faces.

- **Deep Learning**

  This refers to the generation of general-purpose learning algorithms which aid the machine to learn several tasks. A very good example of deep learning can be drawn from Google's AlphaGo project. The AlphaGo once won a complex game against a professional Go player. This was widely thought to be an impossible task before because of the complexity of the game involved.

- **Neural Networks**

  Deep learning occurs when neural networks mimic neurons or brain cells. Artificial neural networks were designed from a biological background. The models make use of the computer science rules to imitate the processes of your human mind, thereby making general learning possible. An artificial neural network attempts to imitate the processes of a highly interconnected human brain cells.

  Neural networks are made up of three key layers, which include the input layer, as well as the hidden layer, and lastly, an output layer. These layers carry a big number of nodes. When an input layer receives information and is given the required weight, the interconnected nodes then multiply the given weight of the connection.

  Once the unit of information has reached the desired level, it passes to the next layer. machines then make comparisons of outputs from neural networks to learn from past experiences. They then make changes affecting connections and weights arising from their differences.

These three key AI terms make it possible for the hardware and the software robots to acquire unique thinking and functions, which are outside the set of codes. Once you have understood these terms, you can then move to a more advanced AI field, which includes the artificial superintelligence, artificial narrow intelligence, and artificial general intelligence.

- **Artificial Intelligence Areas**

  For you to understand the implications of AI on your life and the general society, you need to distinguish the broad types of AI.

- **Artificial Narrow Intelligence (ANI)**

  It is also referred to as the weak AI. It is the type of AI that you are likely to encounter in your world today. This type of AI is programmed to perform single tasks, for example, to check the weather conditions, or play a game like chess. Narrow intelligence can perform real-time tasks once they get information from a specific data set. However, the systems cannot be subjected to perform more than one task at a given time.

  In addition, narrow AI is not like human beings in the sense that they lack emotions associated with humans. They are not also conscious or sentient. Narrow AI can only function within a preset range even though it will appear to you to be complex than that.

  It is much probable that all the machines you see today are narrow AI machines, a good example is, Siri the popular Google Assistant.

  The reason it is called weak is that they are can never be compared to human intelligence. They lack the original intelligence comparable to that of human intelligence.

Although it is referred to as weak intelligence, this should not be a reason for you to take it for granted. ANI systems are designed to process data and very quickly complete the assigned tasks then a normal human being. In this regard, ANI systems have been able to make improvements in the productivity of humans as well as in the quality of life that human beings enjoy.

ANI has also enabled you to get rid of the boring, monotonous tasks that are not enjoyable for you. It has made your lives significantly better. For example, you are now able to escape the frustrations that come with long traffic jams courtesy of self-driving cars or automatic cars. In addition, From the currently available ANI systems, more advanced AI systems are being developed.

- **Artificial General Intelligence**

  Another name for AGI is strong intelligence. AGI refers to machines that have the same intelligence as that of a human brain. They can do any function of your brain. This is the sort of AI that is found in sci-fi movies. The operating systems of AGI machines are not only conscious, but they are also sentient. AGI machines also possess emotional and self-awareness.

  They can process data faster than any human being. AGI is able to make concrete reasoning and can conclusively solve any given problem. They can also make clear judgments. In this regard, ANI is considered to be very good at innovation as well as imagination.

- **Artificial Superintelligence**

  Artificial superintelligence is expected to surpass all human abilities in all areas, including problem solving, creativity, and wisdom. These machines will possess great intelligence never recorded before in human history. It is a type of AI that has got many people worried about the possibility of the human race getting extinct.

How Artificial Intelligence Was Initiated

Scientists have been hard at work for a while now. They were inspired at coming up with machines that have the same intelligence as that of human beings.

The journey started in 1936 when the British mathematician put into practice his theories with the aim of proving that a machine called the Turing machine had the ability to perform tasks similar to those performed by the human brain. He made this possible by breaking down the steps and reprinting them in an algorithm. This was the solid foundation for the establishment of artificial intelligence.

In 1956, a group of scientists came together for a conference at Dartmouth College in New Hampshire. They shared a common agreement that it was possible to learn the key functionalities of the human mind and imitate them into machines. The machine was then given the name, artificial intelligence, by John McCarthy. It was also during this same conference that the scientists developed the first AI program known as a Logic theorist. The program is able to prove several mathematical theorems as well as data.

In 1966, Joseph Weizenbaum came up with a computer program capable of carrying out communication with human beings. He called it ELIZA. ELIZA made use of scripts to imitate various conversations with their counterparts and humans.

In 1972, artificial intelligence entered into the medical field, with MYCIN. This was a system, which was useful in the diagnosis and treatment of various illnesses. They are useful in the diagnosis of diseases as well as in giving out treatment medicine to the patients.

In 1986, the computer acquired the ability to speak. This was made possible by two scientists, namely Terrence J Sejnowski and Charles Rosenberg. They put sample words and phonetical chains to the program, which they then trained to identify the words and correctly pronounced them.

In 1997, an AI chess computer named Deep Blue developed by the IBM Company was able to compete and defeat a reigning world champion. This was widely viewed as a huge success in the field of AI.

In 2011, artificial intelligence made progress into our daily lives. People started interacting extensively with AI-enabled features found in their devices, such as smartphones. The world also witnessed the development of Powerful processors commonly found in your computers or smartphones.

It was in 2011 when a computer program known as Watson competed with human beings in a quiz aired on television. The program surprised many when it won against human competitors. This proved that the computer has the ability to recognize languages and even answer questions in record speed.

And recently, in 2018, the world witnessed a debate between an AI and two master debaters on the complex topic of space travel. It was also in the same year when an AI appointment with a hairdresser. For the entire period, the call lasted, the hairdresser on the other end failed to notice that she was not talking to a human but to a machine.

Advantages and Disadvantages of Using Artificial Intelligence

The advantages of AI include:

- AI Makes minimal errors when compared to the errors that human beings make when subjected to perform the same task. The machines are also able to undertake given tasks fast and accurately.

- Another advantage of AI is that it performs tasks, which are located in hazardous environments. They can perform tasks otherwise viewed as too dangerous for humans to undertake. Such tasks could cause severe injuries or even death to humans.

- They predict the functions you want to be undertaken, for example, when you are typing or searching on your device. They can also guide you on selecting various actions. This way they act as your assistant

- It can be used to detect fraud in card-based systems and as well as possible fraud in other systems.

- AI machines can be useful in your entertainment. Robots are used to enhance various human activities. Some perform entertainment tasks very well.

Disadvantages of AI include:

- It requires a lot of capital to research and comes up with a new AI machine. It also takes a lot of time from the initial stage to launching of an AI machine.

- Some key sectors of the world, such as the human rights groups, have raised pertinent issues touching on AI. They view the advancement of AI as an attempt by humans at creating a fellow human, which is questionable and unethical.

- Access and retrieval of data in AI may not lead to connections in memory like the way human brains function. They cannot also work outside of what they were programmed to do.

- Robots have also been known to replace the jobs done by men. This will lead to massive job losses and will result in economic meltdowns across the globe.

Chapter 2: Robotics

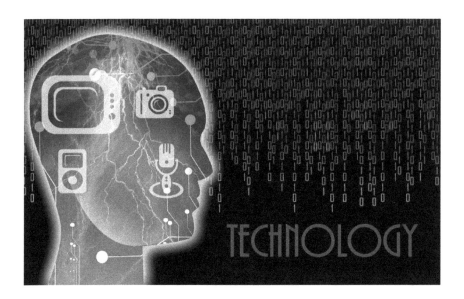

The field of AI has dramatically developed with many new general technological achievements. One advancement is that the rise of Big Data, which offers many possibilities to build programming capability into robotic systems. Another is that the use of the latest varieties of sensors and connected devices to watch environmental aspects like temperature, motion, light, atmospheric pressure, and more. All of these serve AI and, therefore, the generation of a lot of complicated and sophisticated robots for several uses, as well as health, manufacturing, agriculture, safety, and human assist.

The field of robotics additionally intersects with problems around AI. Since robots are physically distinct units, they appear to have their own intelligence, albeit one restricted by their programming and capabilities. This idea has sparked new debates over ancient fictional theories, like Asimov's three laws of AI, that address the interaction of humans with robots in some mechanized future.

Artificial intelligence (AI) is arguably the first exciting field in robotics. It is the foremost controversial. Everyone agrees that a robot would work well in an assembly line; however, there is not any agreement on whether or not a robot will ever be intelligent. Robots are software-driven machines that are sometimes capable of performing a series of actions autonomously or semi-autonomously.

Three vital factors represent a robot:

1. They are programmable.
2. They act with the physical world via actuators and sensors.
3. They are sometimes autonomous or semi-autonomous.

It is said that robots are "usually" autonomous as a result of some robots are not. Telerobots, as an example, is entirely controlled by a human operator; however, robotics continues to be classified as a subsection of AI. This representation can be one instance where the meaning of AI is not entirely clear.

It is tough to get specialists to agree precisely what makes up a robot. Some individuals maintain that a programmable machine should be able to "think" and form decisions. There, however, is no standard definition of "robot thinking." Requiring a tool to "think" infers some level of AI is applied.

Robotics involves designing, programming, and building of actual robots. A minor component of it involves AI. Most AI programs are not applied to create or manage robots. Even once AI is employed to manage robots, machine learning algorithms are solely a section of the more extensive robotic system that additionally includes non-AI programming, actuators, and sensors.

AI involves some level of machine learning, but not always. An example is where innovative design is "trained" to retort to a selected input in a very sure means by use of far-famed inputs and outputs. The critical facet that differentiates AI from a lot of typical programming is that the word "intelligence." Programs that do not involve AI merely perform an outlined sequence of directions. AI programs are built to mimic some degree of human intelligence.

Robots Features

Artificially intelligent robots are the link between AI and robotics. These are machines that are controlled by AI programs. Up until recently, most robots have been programmed to solely perform a series of monotonous tasks. As earlier stated, dull, monotonous activities do not need AI.

Robots need an energy supply, and several factors move into deciding that the style of power provides the foremost freedom and capability for a robotic body. There are many various ways to get, transmit, and store energy. Generators, batteries, and fuel cells provide the power that is regionally kept, however more temporary, whereas tethering to an influence supply naturally curbs the device's independence and variety of functions.

The innovation that empowers automation sense has fostered our ability to speak to machines electronically for several years. Transmission mechanisms, like microphones and cameras, facilitate the transmission of sensory information to computers inside simulated nervous systems. A sense is helpful if not essential to robots' interaction with live, natural phenomena. As the human sensory system is attenuated into vision, hearing, touch, smell, and style- all have already or are in the process of being enforced into robotic technology somehow.

Featured applications of robots include:

- **Computer Vision**

  One obvious application of AI to AI is in computer vision. Computer vision permits robots and drones to explore the physical world much more accurately. This is a technology of AI that the robots use to see. Computer vision plays an important role in the domains of safety, agriculture, health, biometrics, and entertainment.

Computer vision mechanically extracts, analyzes, and comprehends valuable data from one image or an array of pictures. This method involves the development of algorithms to achieve automatic visual understanding.

- **Unsupervised Machine Learning**

Robots are already utilized in manufacturing, however, typically in preprogrammed tasks. Robots may learn tasks with machine learning by being taught by humans or through unsupervised machine learning. While there is a concern that robots like these may replace individuals in industrial jobs, these robots may work alongside humans as "cobots", involving more collaboration with individuals rather than taking up their positions.

Some new robots even can learn in minimal capability. Learning robots acknowledge if a particular action (moving its legs in a specific manner, for instance) achieved the desired result (navigating obstacles). The mechanism stores this data and tries the productive action the subsequent time it encounters an identical scenario. Some robots will learn by mimicking human responses. In Japan, engineers have taught a robot to dance by demonstrating the moves themselves

Intelligence, deftness, sense, and power all converge to create self-governance, that successively may, on paper, cause a virtually personified individualization of mechanical bodies. Derived from its origin inside a piece of speculative fictional tale, the word "robot" has nearly universally observed by artificial means intelligent machinery with a certain degree of humanity to its style and thought (however distant). Therefore, robots are mechanically imbued with a way of individuality. It conjointly raises several potential queries on whether or not or not a machine will ever incredibly "awaken" and become aware, and by extension, treated as a person (or personal subject).

- **Human Error**

  Another primary application of AI to robotics that has gotten attention in recent years is autonomous or self-driving cars. This sort of use is enticing because it promises to reduce human driver error that is the cause of most traffic accidents. A robotic automobile will not get tired, impaired, or inattentive while the human driver will. Even though there are several high-profile accidents involving autonomous vehicles, they show plenty of promise to be considered safer than human-driven cars.

  A significant area of analysis involving robots and AI is in medical technologies. Robots within the future might perform surgery without intervention from a doctor. Like autonomous vehicles, robotic surgeons might perform delicate operations for extended periods than human doctors will, while not feeling tired or making mistakes.

- **Dexterity**

  Dexterity is the practicality of organs, limbs, and extremities, likewise because of the general varies of motor ability and physical capability of an animated body. In robotics, quickness is maximized wherever there is harmony between high-level programming and subtle hardware that comes with environmental sensing capability. Several alternative companies are achieving important milestones in robotic quickness and physical interactivity. This technology application lends an excellent deal of insight into the longer term of robot quickness. However, not all robots mimic the human physical type (those that do are usually mentioned as "androids," whose Greek chronicle origin essentially interprets as "likeness to man").

Classification of Robots

The most popular robot classification includes immobile and mobile robots. These two types have entirely different operating systems and thus have different capabilities. A majority of **Fixed robots** are industrial robot operators who work in well-outlined environments tailored for programmable machines. Industrial robots perform specific and dull tasks such as bonding or painting elements in automotive manufacturing factories. With the development of human-robot interaction devices and sensors, robot operators are more and more used in a minimally controlled setting like surgery, which requires high precision.

In comparison, **mobile robots** maneuver around and carry out multiple tasks in considerably vast, ill-defined, and unforeseeable environments that do not seem to be designed explicitly for robots. These robots have to modify things that do not seem to be precisely renowned but which change over time. Environments like these will embody unpredictable entities like humans and animals. Some of the common mobile robots include robotic gutter cleaners and automated self-driving vehicles.

There lacks a clear distinction between the functions meted out by mobile robots and immobile robots. There exist three primary **environments** for which mobile robots would need considerably variable class principles as a result of the difference in the means of **motion**: *terrestrial* (for instance, cars), *aquatic* (for instance, underwater expedition), and *aerial* (for instance, drones). The classification is not strict; take, for instance, some amphibious robots that move on water and the ground. Robots that operate in these three terrains are further subdivided into pseudo groups: terrestrial robots either have legs, or wheels, and aerial drones are light balloons or heavy craft, that are successively sub-grouped into fixed-wing and rotary-wing as in the case of helicopters.

Nowadays, robots do plenty of various tasks in several industries, and therefore the variety of jobs entrusted to robots is growing steadily. Robots can also be grouped in accordance with the supposed **application** industry and the functions they perform as follows:

- **Industrial robots** that perform repetitive duties on manufacturing tasks are mentioned. Industrial robots are robots employed in industrial manufacturing surroundings. Sometimes these are articulated arms developed explicitly for applications such as assembling, product handling, painting et al. If we tend to decide strictly by uses of this kind, we might additionally embrace some automatic guided vehicles and different robots. The first robots are said to have been industrial robots as a result of the well-defined surroundings simplified their style.

- **Service robots**, alternatively, assist humans in their tasks. Domestic or social robots include several quite wholly different devices like robotic sweepers, vacuum cleaners, gutter cleaners, robotic pool cleaners, and various robots that may do completely different chores. To add, defense applications like intelligence activity drones and telepresence robots can be thought to be home robots if employed in that environment. Service robots do not constitute different varieties by usage. These can also be completely different information-gathering robots, robots created to indicate off technologies, robots used for analysis, etc.

Robots have also been increasingly used in the medical field, in surgeries, training, and rehabilitation. These are examples of applications that need sharper sensors and better user interaction. **Medical robots** are employed in drugs and medical establishments. The very first medical application being surgery robots.

- **Military robots** are employed in the military. These kinds of robots include explosive diffusion robots, transportation robots, and intelligence activity drones. Usually, robots created at first for military functions will be employed in law enforcement, search and rescue efforts, and different connected fields.

- **Entertainment robots** used for recreation. This is often an inclusive class. It starts with toy bots like Robosapien or the running grandfather clock and culminates with real heavyweights like articulated robot arms used as movement simulators. Hobby robots are also in this class. They constitute those that you create for the sake of code. Line tracker robots, sumo-bots, are robots created only for fun and competition purposes.

- **Space robots** would come with robots used on the International Space Station. Mars rovers and different robots employed in space exploration.

The Three Laws of Robotics

In fiction, the three laws of robotics are a collection of 3 rules written by Isaac Asimov, introduced in his short work of fiction in 1942 the rules go as follows:

1. "A robot may not injure a person or, through inaction, permit a person to come to harm."

2. "A robot should adapt orders passed by persons except when the aforementioned orders would conflict with the First Law."

3. "A robot should defend its own existence as long in and of itself protection does not conflict with the primary or Second Law."

Asimov's laws are an endeavor to handle the AI-uprising threat. The technical obstacle in creating robots abide by them is our current limitation in making them observe the commandments. The major obstacle, a philosophical and moral one, is our assumption that given such imprecise constraints, the robots can behave specifically however we would like them to, even though we do not understand what we tend to mean.

Chapter 3: Software and Programming to Make Predictions and Intelligent Decisions

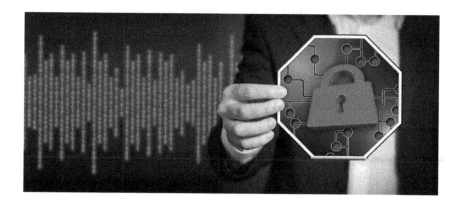

Artificial intelligence has made substantial progress into every part of your life, and this is projected to continue in the near future. AI has made possible for automation of tasks for you as a user, which has enabled you to have a unique experience as you interact with your normal devices such as the smartphone. Automating these processes saves you of your time and energy and makes your job easier allowing you or your employees to work more efficiently and productively.

AI software provides developers with tools to build intelligent applications. The tools include algorithms, and libraries, or frameworks of code, which is useful in the creation of important functionalities for the software. AI software enables you to be more productive, enabling you to carry out otherwise boring and monotonous tasks using your AI machine. It also helps companies in coming up with key decisions.

AI software is also used by software professionals to come up with solutions which are beneficial to workers in all kind of professions. Software applications are important when generating new applications. They can also help you to improve on any existing software application. Moreover, you can also use AI software to carry out general machine learning capabilities or deep learning capabilities

Importance of AI Software

Some of the significance of AI software are:

- **Useful in creating conversational interfaces**

  Various Software companies are striving to improve and compete with the latest development in AI in order to come up with competitive AI products like Amazon's Alexa or Google Home a use AI software.

- **AI software helps in personalization**

  You can create a high level of personalization by using machine learning algorithms. Personalization improves your software products for all users; thus, you offer them a unique experience. Companies that have successfully used AI in personalization includes Amazon, which uses the software to personalize their consumer shopping and Netflix in their movie recommendation capabilities.

- **AI software useful in intelligent decision making**

  AI helps humans to make logical assumptions instead of the other way round. Machine learning is important for you when making decisions touching on your business because it provides you with evidence and predicted consequences of the decision you are making. You are enabled then to avoid costly human errors. It can also help equip users with the information necessary to defend the decisions they make.

- **Predictive capabilities**

  The predictive feature provides outcomes which the platforms take to be right. For example, in business, you can use the software to have expense management applications add an expense to you repost on its own. You can easily insert this kind of application with your AI software.

- **AI software is useful in the automation of monotonous tasks**

  You can use machine learning in automating challenging tasks that you do on a daily basis in your workplace. By using AI for these tasks, you save a lot of time, which you can use to carry out other more productive tasks. Of importance is the fact that contrary to popular beliefs, AI use does not replace human jobs, but it serves to complement them.

Artificial Intelligence Software Types

The types of Artificial intelligence is quite wide. There are key categories of AI, such as chatbot, AI platforms, deep learning, and machine learning, which you should know.

- **Deep learning**

  Deep learning makes predictions and decisions using a neural network. With artificial neural networks, important decisions are made in the same way in which the human mind normally makes decisions.

- **Machine learning**

  This algorithm category consists of a wide variety of frameworks performing various functions from the available data. They, however, require some element of personal training. You require enough training and experience to incubate an intelligent application using a machine learning algorithm.

- **Chatbots**

  Chatbots are an advance area of AI learning. They are created to perform a specific function, for example, for automation in business and to help in creating a unique customer experience. The applications interact with customers using voice or texts.

  Chatbots can also be used in call centers by agents. It can also be used to carry out live chats with potential customers. Businesses can also determine customer need by using chatbots.

  Moreover, chatbots are often used as tools for customer support or virtual assistance. Chatbots can interact with customers over a long time. This way, as they interact, they also learn new vocabulary and intelligence.

- **AI platforms**

  AI platforms give you good solutions, especially if you are trying to build your applications using another platform. These tools give you a drag and drop option to assist you in building the app from zero. The platforms equip applications with an intelligent advantage; they possibly make the creation of smart applications less costly and fast. However, you will need to be highly skilled and knowledgeable to maneuver through the platforms.

- **AI programming for the beginners**

  Artificial intelligence refers to the branch computer science that involves the development of machines with similar intelligence as that of humans. Artificial intelligence experts were interested in coming up with systems that are unique and which could surpass human intelligence. The advancement in technology has made it possible to create self-aware robots, which will become part of your life in the coming days.

The Goals of AI

Some of the goals of AI are specific. This includes reasoning, planning, and scheduling, natural language processing (NLP), among others.

- **Knowledge and reasoning**— The main goal of AI is to focus on the implementation and designing of computer representations, with the aim of processing information. AI automates different types of reasoning through the use of codification of relationships so that they can be interpreted easily by the computer system. Knowledge representation and reasoning are usually applied in a natural-language user interface that facilitates communication between computers and humans.

- **Automated planning and scheduling**—AI is also concerned with the generation of automated action sequences, which corresponds to AI systems measurements. The goal of AI is to mechanize and automate the generation of planned actions through planning and scheduling. One of the examples of AI planning is the self-correcting robots that act as computerized suggestions.

- **Natural language processing (NLP)**— Another goal of AI is to process natural language. NLP entails an analysis and generation of language that can be used for computer interfacing. The NLP process aims to implement specific computer systems that can be used to process big data.

- **Computer vision**— The main aim of the AI component is to assess the automation and computerization of activities, which can be performed by system development to process and interpret visual data. Computer vision utilizes several applications such as object recognition, video tracking, and automated image manipulation. Computer vision is commonly applied in automated image manipulation, object recognition, virtual reality integration, and video tracking.

- **Robotics**—Another significant goal of AI is to construct, design, and operate robots and machines that can replace human tasks. Robotics refers to the scientific branch that entails electronic engineering, computer science, information engineering, and electronic engineering. Research on robotics is currently conducted to promote military, domestic, and commercial applications.

Through these goals, AI has greatly influenced a wide variety of sectors, including education, transport, security, infrastructure, and communication.

Classification of AI

There are three common categories of AI-based on their capabilities:

- **Weak Artificial intelligence**

  Weak AI is also known as Narrow AI. It was designed to undertake a single task. You cannot find any real intelligence in weak AI. You can't also find any self-awareness with weak AI. A good example of a weak AI is iOS Siri.

- **Strong AI**

  It is also referred to as True AI. The software performs like the human brain. It undertakes tasks which a normal human can do. A good example of a strong AI is the Matrix I Robot.

- **Artificial superintelligence**

  This is an intellect that can perform better than the best human brains in all areas, including scientific creativity and social skills. Because of advancements in artificial superintelligence, many people have raised concerned about the possibility of human beings becoming extinct and being replaced by super-intelligent robots.

How to Get Started as an AI Beginner

As a beginner in understanding how AI works, it is essential that you follow the steps below:

- **Step 1: Learn a programming language**

  Learning the programming languages is one of the first steps you need to undertake. It is advisable to start with programmers like Python. Python programming language is important because it is suited to machine learning. We will discuss the python program in detail and the other programs that can help you get started in your AI in our subsequent subtopics.

- **Step 2: Learn about machine learning**

  You also need to delve into the world of machine learning. Get to know what it is all about and its importance.

- **Step 3: Take part in contests**

  If possible, you needed to register and take part in any AI or BOT programming workshops or contests within your vicinity. If you cannot find any consider looking for some on the internet.

Reinforcement Learning: Programming Languages for Artificial Intelligence You Need to Know

There are several AI programming languages that are beneficial to you and which you need to know. These includes:

- **Lisp**

  It is a mathematical notation designed for computer programs. It is based on lambda calculus. The program is used to manipulate source code to give rise to rise to macro systems that enable you to come up with new syntax.

- **Smalltalk**

  Small talk is useful in machine learning and in the generation of genetic algorithms. It is also useful in neural networks and simulations.

- **Prolog**

  Prolog programming language is used for symbol reasoning and database. It also a very popular application with AI experts today.

- **Python**

  Python is one of the most popular programming languages which AI researchers use today. Python can be used with packages for applications such as Machine Learning, and Natural Language Processing. It can also be used with Neural Networks. One key advantage of Python language is that it can be used with various programming paradigms.,

- **C ++**

    C++ is a very popular language program with AI researchers today. The software is a general-purpose programming language created as an extension of the popular C programming language or C with classes. The programming language has grown with time in functionality. Today's C++ complex in nature and is equipped with object-oriented, functional features. It has facilities for low-level memory manipulation. This programming language is often implemented as a compiled language. In addition, the vendors of this program provide C++ compilers such as the Free Software Foundation and IBM.

    C++ was created to favor system programming. C++ has at least one main function. When using the program, you are allowed to divide your code into separate functions but ensure each function is performing a particular task.

    You as a compiler should be able to know the functions name, parameters as well as return type. You can also get various inbuilt functions from the C++ library, which enables your program to call.

- **Java**

    Java is another popular general-purpose programming language with the researchers today. The program is class-based and object-oriented. The program is specifically designed to carry out a few implementation dependencies. With Java, you, as a developer, are enabled to write once and run anywhere-WORA. This will enable you to run your compiled Java application on all platforms that support Java without the need for you to do a recompilation. Some of the latest versions of Java program include the popular Java 13, released in 2019, and Java 11, which hit the market in 2018.

Key Softwares That Are Used for Predictive Purposes

Your career can benefit greatly from the predictive analysis. It can be used to improve overall productivity in your workplace. It is also useful in a reduction of business risks as well as in the detection of possible fraud even before it happens. Predictive analysis is also used to identify and address client expectations in business. This will give you a clear lead ahead of your competitors. Such intelligence is of great help to your business especially when you are generating business strategies. You should, therefore, look for the proper tools to implement them for you to benefit. Here are some of the important predictive analysis software available for you today.

- **SiSense**

    This is a software designed to be used by companies of various sizes. The advantage of this software is that it is user-friendly. You also get various business analytic features that will aid you in staying ahead of the competition. The software has the capability of carrying out data preparations that are complex in nature. They make the data easy for your understanding and enable you to use them to make key business decisions faster.

- **Microsoft R open**

    The software is an open-source platform that specializes in the analysis of statistics and data science. The software was specifically created on the statistical language R-3.5.0. The platform can be used with various packages, applications, or scripts. Some of the popular applications that work with this platform are Windows OS and Linux.

- **Microsoft Azure Machine Learning Studio**

  This is one of the popular platforms used for predictive analytics by AI researchers and other software experts. The platform makes use of data science and as well as cloud-based tools to help you come up with complete reports based on different types of available data. With this platform, you are able to create, use, and share predictive analytics solutions fast and easy. This software is great for startups and small companies.

- **Oracle Crystal Ball**

  The platform makes use of its spreadsheet-based application to make predictive modeling or forecasting. It is also used in simulation as well as in optimization. The platform is best suited for strategic planners or financial analysts. This platform is quite popular with software engineers and other scientists.

Chapter 4: Jobs and Careers After the AI Revolution

The artificial intelligence revolution toughly inclined the biosphere of toil in the 21st epoch. PCs, procedures, and software streamline daily errands, and you cannot imagine how you could accomplish most things devoid of them. Nevertheless, is it also incredible to visualize how you could grip most dealing outpaces without the humanoid workforce? What is by now unblemished and assured is that first-hand technical enlargements will devise an essential impression on the international employment marketplace inside the succeeding limited ages, not just on manufacturing jobs, but on the fundamental of humanoid errands? The following are various application areas after the AI revolution.

Philosophy

Philosophy is a very important field as it attempts to answer important critical thinking questions like can a machine act intelligently? Can it solve like a human being? Is computers' intelligence like human ones? For example, the viewpoint of A, where A is a discipline, comprises theorists scrutinizing the perceptions of A and occasionally commenting on coherent and non-coherent concepts. Artificial brainpower has nearby precise acquaintances with the way of life than other disciplines because it segments numerous conceptions with thinking, like action, awareness, epistemology (what it is serviceable to say about the biosphere), and even open will. The thinking of a most regularly encompasses guidance to the consultants of A nearly what they can and cannot do.

The AI point of assessment is that ethical philosophies are convenient to AI only if they don't inhibit human-level simulated organizations and arrange for a foundation for scheming arrangements with views, go perceptive, and proposal. AI investigation has principally highlighted validating the activities accessible in a state of affairs, and the concerns of enchanting each of numerous activities. To do this, AI has mainly dispensed with pretentious estimates to sensations.

Mathematics

Mathematics is used to write the logic and an algorithm for machine learning. Philosophy thinks and defines a particular intelligence and the way it should work. But here comes the intelligence of Mathematicians to come out with calculations and algorithms for learning. Good knowledge of mathematics is a necessary imperative skill to develop a model of AI. For example, Earl Stanhope's Sense Presenter was a mechanism that was capable of resolving syllogisms, mathematical complications in a rational formula, and straightforward inquiries of likelihood.

In 1815-1864, George Boole brought together his recognized linguistic for creating reasonable insinuation in Boolean algebra. In 1848-1925, Gottlob Frege created a sense that is fundamentally the first-order sense that nowadays forms the utmost basic understanding demonstration scheme. Between 1906 and 1978, Kurt Gödel displayed that there are restrictions on what sense can do. His Incompleteness Statement exposed that in any official reasoning potent abundantly to define the possessions of ordinary figures, there are true testimonials a procedure cannot establish whose truth. And in 1995, Roger Penrose attempts to demonstrate that a humanoid concentration has non-computable competencies.

Computer Science

Computer science is an academic discipline offered in contemporary colleges and universities. A Computer scientist writes the codes for making the neural network for artificial intelligence. It then updates the values or properties of the neural network based on the data provided to the system. You achieve Artificial Intelligence this way. Historically, you base its speculative tradition upon the long-standing behaviors of representative reasoning, calculation, and the moderately more current enlargements in electrical commerce. It was, nevertheless, the speculative toil of the statistician Alan Turing in the 1930s and instigating his philosophy by the statistician John von Neumann in the initial 1950s that tip to the expansion of the modem stored-program PC.

Psychology

Modern Psychology is the discipline that educates how the concentration maneuvers, how do we perform, and how our I.Q.s progress data. It is used to study and find thinking of humans and animals. This discipline enables data science to understand the Brain, Behavior, and Person essential to make things like the human brain. Linguistic is a vital part of humanoid intellect. Much of the primary work on acquaintance illustration links to linguistic and well-versed by inquiries into dialectology. It is normal for us to use the indulgent of how humanoid, and other animals IQs tip to intellectual conduct in the pursuit to build artificial brainpower schemes. Equally, it takes intelligence to discover the possessions of simulated schemes to test the suggestions regarding human schemes. Many sub-fields of AI are instantaneously constructing replicas of how the human scheme activates, and synthetic schemes for resolving real-world glitches, and are permitting valuable thoughts to handover amongst them.

Neuroscience

Tens of billions of neurons make up the brain for each attached to hundreds or thousands of further neurons. For each neuron is a pretentious handling maneuver, e.g., just firing or not firing provisional on the overall sum of action nurturing into it. Nevertheless, outsized links of neurons are authoritative computational maneuvers that can study how top to function. The arena of Connectionism or Neural Links tries to construct synthetic schemes centered on shortened links of streamlined synthetic neurons. The objective is to create dominant AI systems and replicas of numerous human aptitudes. Neural links work at a sub-symbolic level, however much of the cognizant human perceptive seems to function at a figurative level. Synthetic neural links execute well as many modest errands and offer moral replicas of utmost human aptitudes. However, there are numerous errands they are not so virtuous at, and other methods appear more auspicious in those zones.

Ontology

It is the training of the types of possessions that are present. In AI, the curriculums, and stretches contract with countless varieties of substances, and we learn what these categories are and what their elementary belongings are. Prominence on ontology started in the 1990s.

Heuristics

A heuristic is a way of exasperating to determine roughly or a hint entrenched in a package. You use the tenure variously in AI. You can also use heuristic functions in some methodologies to pursuit the quantity of how faraway a protuberance in a pursuit tree appears to be from an objective. Heuristic establishes that equate two nodes in a pursuit tree to see if one is restored than the former, i.e., create up an advance in the direction of the goal and maybe more worthwhile.

Will AI Replace Jobs?

The panic over AI replacing tons of human jobs is misinforming. AI cannot replace jobs. Well, not 100 percent. The work of machines will replace not every specific occupation, but machines will perform some individuals' occupational activities. For instance, the risk of a barkeeper being interchanged is very high. Already today, it is theoretically practical that a machinelike mechanism could blend drinks, direct the clients' orders straight to the kitchenette, collect criticisms, and assent the clients' cash. The mesosphere in the inns or the cafés will no longer be similar. Because of the shortage of approval by probable consumers and the great acquirement costs, it is convinced that a huge percent of all barkeepers will not drop their careers in the succeeding few ages. However, they recognize that no job is safe. The question should not be whether it will change the workplace. The real question should be how companies can successfully use it in ways that help makes humans faster, productive, and more efficient. This will make jobs shift and evolve, not disappear. It will augment how to people complete their work by doing things such as pulling and analyzing data to aid in real-time decision-making. An example of this might be how AI could empower a customer service agent with information from a CRM platform to help the agent decide whether to issue a refund.

A skills gap will emerge among human employees. It will convey many aids in the arrangement of higher efficiency, GDP growth, enhanced commercial concert, and new affluence, but they will also adjust the services essential of human employees. With AI automating repeatable and mundane tasks from accounting to the assembly line, the skill set of the human workforce needs to evolve. The focus and responsibilities of the average employee will widen and deepen. People will need to have a wealth of knowledge and more skills. Essentially, they will need to be great at doing a lot of things.

You need to think about educating our current, and future workforce to learn the skills that AI cannot replace, including:

- **Social skills**: AI will find it is hard to have intercultural sensitivity. They cannot be good at being a leader, cannot take part in a brainstorm or do interpersonal interactions. Cognitive skills: AI is less effective when it has to make judgments based on the specific data on which they have trained it. In the real world, people often decide about situations that do not have previously faced. The problem lies in systems that can match data, but not understand its significance. Skills like complex problem solving, reasoning, negotiating, and decision-making will be important for human workers.

- **Emotional Skills**: AI technology is far from being able to replicate empathy, adaptability, and other emotional skills. Think about this in the form of health care. While AI is empowering doctors and nurses with information to help them decide and complete various tasks, the human touch and conversation with a doctor will always remain important. To come across the perfect principles set for the Commerce forthcoming, personnel must learn new significant recommendations, but they requisite also adapt the educational system to this new context situations. An arrangement at the World Economic Forum states that both schools and universities should not instill the biosphere as it was, but as it will be. They, then, need new stipulation approaches for specific nations. They must inspire scholars' concern in topics like calculation, material knowledge, discipline, and expertise when they are still in school, and tutors with numerical proficiency must impart scholars how to contemplate judgmentally when by means of new broadcasting and help them accomplish a necessary hold of new digital and material strategies.

Creative Jobs

Creative professions have advanced in current eras, and machines will not replace humans in these professions in the upcoming years either. Whether they are celebrities with their tune, performers with their works or writers and thespians with their legendary, or photographic works, or humankind and broadcasting intellectuals, the projection accumulative mandate for their occupations. Mechanism knowledge, as the most powerful branch of artificial intelligence, can only achieve tedious errands by imitating facts and succeeding instructions. It cannot take part in a brainstorm, think creatively, or tackle novel situations, e.g., situations it hasn't encountered before.

Humans can write an emotionally compelling story or soothe a frustrated customer with a personalized conversation, Humans are proactive, and AI is reactive. Humans take a long rational perceptive, passionate aptitude, and a non-linear method to work and life unbearable for AI to attain. That's the bottommost line. The fact relics that AI can't adjust or generate the way people do. AI isn't skillful in identifying novel shapes and new manners or exceptionally grants them. Consequently, there is a level of humanoid originality and complexity required to accomplish and construct upon all software submissions.

In the forthcoming, the end-user will still mandate resourceful showbiz selections and realistically alluring performances. Ever since you encompass no mundane, gifted software can scarcely perform these professions. The alike relate to the systematic expansive sector or occupations with an emotive element. The announcement with other persons will continually come right from individuals. Communication gradually takes place in communal links, but you have to maintain and technically equip them. This is the central challenge of Industry.

Careers in AI and Data Science in The Future

Experts expect Artificial intelligence and data science will be responsible for the most significant and disruptive innovations cutting across the various sectors. AI scientists will play some key roles in this area. One of these roles will be for the scientists to come up with a high-level research-oriented work which surpasses the normally available techniques. Businesses will strive to be part of this action by investing heavily in algorithm-based platforms that assures them an added advantage in the competitive market. This may mean the businesses will apply machine learning at higher levels than we see today.

Moreover, more people will be holders of PhDs and masters' degrees, just like the way we find a big population of MBA graduates today. You should also expect conservative businesses and industries to automate some of their key functions to create a high tech-oriented company culture as well as in their hiring profiles. If the companies fail to embrace this technology, they will miss out on the advantages that come with machine learning. As the designing and improvement of AI machines advance each passing day, experts are already predicting that the economic activities will be disrupted in a big way.

It is also a known fact that AI systems take a big chunk of data as compared to humans. The implication of this is that you might be forced to change your career in the next near future. Although it is expected for the AI to make some jobs and careers better, one cannot ignore the fact that most jobs will be declared absolute by this technology. AI will link the customer to the service or the product, thereby cutting various jobs that exist in between.

What to Study? Artificial Intelligence Operating System

What is an artificial intelligence operating system? well, this is a system that is used to manage the computer software and as well as the hardware. It also helps in providing a common service necessary for the computer or a machine to generate a solution for a complex problem easily. It is expected that artificial intelligence will be playing key functions in operating systems of computers, devices, and other machines. The benefits of AI-based operating systems is quite immense. Key fields such as academic, defense, medical, research, scientific, are expected to benefit from this technological development.

You, therefore, need to be part of the action in order to benefit because the AI learning process is expected to be part of us for the unforeseeable future. Once the development of OS based on AI is complete, it could make your life much more interesting as it will help you perform expert tasks, and monotonous, boring tasks that you normally don't enjoy doing. Another benefit of AIOS is that the computer crashes that you often encounter will be greatly reduced. Besides, the time to execute an operation using AIOS would be much shorter as compared to the time it normally takes in a normal OS.

Moreover, artificial intelligence salaries are incomparable to none. It is one of the fattest paychecks you rarely find even in the most coveted careers. This is because careers in AI are highly competitive and calls for rare specialist talent. To locate such talent is almost an impossible task, that is why possessing such talent will make you a much sought after professional.

Currently, a professional in the field of AI is able to take home a salary ranging from an average of between $100,000-180,000 per annum. This, however, can higher depending on the uniqueness of your qualifications and giftings.

Is Data Science A Good Career?

Yes, data science is a good career. Data science, as the science of extracting insights from data along with domain knowledge, helps in strategic decision-making, leading to better customer experience, reduced costs, and higher profits. With so many data around, governments, corporates, brands, etc. are getting pressure on how to make sense of it and how to use it for more efficient functioning and profits. Data Science is the answer to this challenge.

A data scientist structures big volumes of data then subject it to data analysis. This entails researching both the data and as well as their origin and structure. It is done basically to strengthen the data set, which is incomplete. It is also used to create links between one abstract data set and the other. The work of a big data developer is majorly to deal with the set-up and processing, as well as the storage of vast unstructured data volumes belonging to large companies and governments. On the other hand, data artists are charged with the responsibility of graphic presentation and editing of data volumes.

Although data scientist career is relatively new, its importance cannot be gainsaid. It is one of the very important careers in the field of communication and science today. It is widely expected that this new career will be one of the hottest and well remunerated in the near future. If you are considering pursuing a career in this field, then it is advisable that you acquire key IT skills that will help you maneuver through the complex demands of the career. You need to be adept in the relevant programming languages. You should also have the necessary knowledge and skills to write complex programming codes. It is also helpful if you familiarize yourself with the business processes of the corporate world in order for you to create reasonable links. Furthermore, you need to acquire basic knowledge in business fields such as business administration, economics, and marketing. Besides, it will help your career if you cultivate rich interpersonal qualities.

A data scientist is expected to offer quality services, which meet the expectations of their customers as well as those of the employer. For you to be successful in this field, you must receive the requisite training that makes you highly competent and effective. During the course of your work as a data scientist, you are expected to perform data processing as well as the computation on big scales. For you to be adept in this, consider getting training from the relevant institutions. Such training entails some knowledge in engineering, mathematical sciences, and social sciences.

Computing and Artificial Intelligence

Computing systems make use of machine learning and natural language processing. It also makes use of AI data mining methods. However, computing systems doesn't stop there; it strives to imitate the key functionaries of the human brain on a machine. It makes use of available data to make key decisions, just like the way human beings make logical decisions. Once it is through with its analysis, computing systems, for example, IBM then gives its best alternative to a given problem at hand. This might not be the right choice; it is, therefore, upon you to decide the appropriate course of action is in a given situation.

The key difference between computing platforms and artificial intelligence systems is that AI is created to carry out some tasks on your behalf while the computing system serves the purpose of giving you the advice you need or the guidance you need before making key decisions.

Businesses can use the platform to come up with risk factors needed before a decision is made. The platform provides companies with a recommendation on investments as well as other key business decisions. The opportunities offered by this technology is huge and is largely untapped.

Chapter 5: Artificial Intelligence Algorithms

Over the past years, algorithms were believed to be a subject for mathematicians and computer scientists. However, with the recent technological advancements and the rapid evolution of artificial intelligence, it has become necessary for everyone to have a glimpse of what algorithms entail. AI has been in the present-day adopted in almost all areas of operations, including hotels and hospitals, where it is used to make human activities easy by using machines to handle complex tasks.

What then does the term algorithm in AI mean? An algorithm is a basic set of rules that are followed mainly by computers in carrying out calculations or handling other problem-solving operations. The goal of an algorithm is basically to solve a problem using the simplest way possible and within a short time by following a predetermined procedure or set of steps. You can also view algorithms as shortcuts that help you give instructions to your computer. By adopting the use of these algorithms, you communicate to a computer by telling it what action to take next using statements which are denoted by "and," "not" and "or." These statements guide the computer in handling problems, just like a human being would have done. Most of the algorithms resemble mathematical problems, which begin as easy tasks with increasing levels of complexity as they are expounded. The simple steps you follow in your house when baking your favorite cake depicts a simple form of an algorithm.

With the growth of the AI sector in trying to bridge the gap that exists between human and machine capabilities, it is essential to understand the various algorithms used in AI. It is, however, necessary to note that not all algorithms are applied in artificial intelligence. The commonly used algorithms here are:

- Convolutional Neural Networks (CNNs)

- Recurrent Neural Networks (RNNs)

- Reinforcement Learning (RL)

You may be wondering what is meant by the term neural networks in algorithms. This should not send chills down your spine because this chapter contains a detailed outline of everything you may want to know concerning algorithms and their applications in AI. Neural networks are a unique set of well-defined algorithms that are tailored to resemble a human brain with the ability to recognize patterns efficiently. The designs they recognize are usually in numerical form and contained in vectors in which all data such as sound, image, and text must be translated. These neural networks interpret sensory data through perception, labeling, as well as clustering of raw input. Different types of neural networks have various functions, such as clustering and classification of data based on the similarities depicted.

Before getting into the types of algorithms, you need first to understand the essential layers found in a simple neural network.

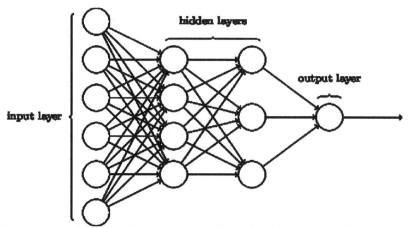

Figure 1: The architecture of a simple neural network

Input layer - here, you input data for your model. The amount of neurons introduced here is similar to the number of features present in the data in the output layer. For instance, the sum of pixels in case you are using an image.

Hidden layer -it is a layer that comes directly after the input layer. Based on the algorithm model as well as the data size, the number of hidden layers may be more than one with each one of them containing a different amount of neurons that are more than the sum of features in the output layer.

Output layer - contains output generated from all the hidden layers. The output information is manipulated using sigmoid logistic as well as softmax functions that convert each output class into a probability score of the representative type.

Convolution Neural Networks (CNNs or ConvNet)

CNN is an algorithm that can take the input, for example, an image, allocate weights to its various features, and still be in a position to differentiate the aspects from each other. The pre-processing elements required in CNNs tends to be lower in comparison to those required for other forms of algorithms. Additionally, with sufficient training, CNNs can learn the various types of filters rather than having to hand-engineer them as it is the case with other types of algorithms.

The design of CNN is made to resemble the connectivity of brain neurons in a human being. This architectural design is based on the organization of the human visual cortex. Within your visual cortex, different neurons react in response to varying stimuli within a restricted section of your visual field, referred to as the receptive field.

Layers Found in ConvNets

ConvNets are made of sequential layers, with each layer transforming the input data from one volume to another by the use of differentiable functions. The primary role played by the ConvNets is to minimize the size of an image into a smaller form that is easy to process while still maintaining its critical features. Below are the common layers found in CNNs.

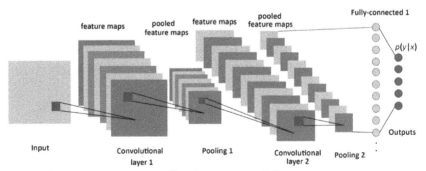

Figure 2: A sample CNNs architecture set up

Input layer - this contains the raw data input, that in most cases, is usually an image. Let's assume that your input is an image of volume 32*32*3

Convolution layer - this forms the core building block of a CNN where all the complex computations are done. Here, the output volume is computed between filters as well as image patches. The amount of filters used determines the depth of the resultant output volume. Suppose you use a total of 12 filters, then the size of your output will be 32*32*12.

Pool layer - This layer is added in the model with the sole purpose of lowering the overall volume of the data under computation. There are basically two types of pooling that are; maximum pooling as well as average pooling with maximum pooling being commonly used in CNNs. Maximum pooling suggests that the maximum element be pooled. For example, in your illustration, if you use a maximum pool containing filters of 2*2 and a stride of 2, then the resulting output volume will change to16*16*12. There may be several pooling layers based on the size of the entire computation.

Fully connected layer - contains the input generated from all other segments, and it computes output volumes of class scores in sizes that are equal to the respective sum of classes.

CNN's are applied in various areas of AI, including image processing and others such as:

- **Text recognition** - CNN has been adopted in decoding visual images in texts through a function known as optical character recognition (OCR).

- **Facial recognition** - apart from image recognition and processing, CNN has also been used in the field of facial recognition. Recently, it has been seen to handle the task of recognizing faces from different angles, even when the visibility is limited.

Recurrent Neural Networks (RNNs)

Anytime you are thinking. You do not start the process from scratch. Whatever you think, comes from some information that already exists in your mind. Similarly, as you continue reading through this chapter, you will understand some words, based on your previous encounter with them. This simply means that you do not discard all the information you have in mind once you are done using it, but instead, you store it for future use. This simply means that output from one process may be used as input for another process. This is the concept behind which RNNs operates.

RNNs is an artificial intelligence algorithm that uses the output information from a previous layer as input in the current layer. Here, the input, as well as the output vectors from the different steps, are dependent. Just as the name recurrent suggests, the dependent input and output keep on being used over and over again. That is, they recur. This type of algorithm is primarily used in language processing and speech recognition, where it recognizes the sequential characteristics of data and uses specific patterns to predetermine the next probable action. The traditional forms of algorithm considered the inputs and the outputs to be independent variables. This, however, posed a challenge, especially where a prediction of the next action or step is required. RNNs were developed to bridge this gap through its unique feature, which is the hidden layer, which acts as a memory to remember certain bits of information concerning a sequence. RNNs can accommodate more than one input vector and work on them to produce one or more outputs based on the weights as well as biases applied.

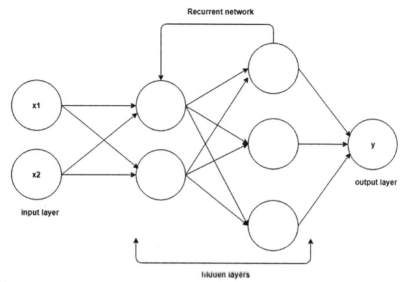

Figure 3: A typical architecture of RNNs

The hidden layer remembers all the previously handled information. RNNs adopts the use of a similar parameter for every input while still performing a similar task for the rest of the input sequences to bring out the output or outputs. The chain-like nature of the RNNs shows that there exists a relationship between the sequences and lists of the various inputs. The RNNs poses a feature which makes them more preferred for use than the CNNs, that is they allow you to operate over a series of vectors in the input or output layer or in general cases both layers unlike the CNNs where they only accept a fixed size of vector input and produce a fixed volume of vector output.

How Does RNNs Work?

To help you understand how the RNNs works, here is an illustration.

Assume that you are working on an input network consisting of one layer of input, two hidden layers, as well as a single output layer. Every hidden layer has specific biases as well as weights applied to them, for example, hidden layer 1has weight 1 (w1) and Bias 1 (b1) while hidden layer 2 has (w2 and b2). This shows that the two hidden layers operate under different weights as well as biases and are thus independent of each other. This independent character means that the second hidden layer does not rely on the output from the first hidden layer. Such a scenario, therefore, does not qualify under the RNN.

When the RNN model is introduced, the following happens:

The independent activations will be converted to dependent activations by adding similar weights as well as biases in the hidden layers. This means that the output from the first layer will be used as the input in the subsequent hidden layer. By converting the activations from independent to dependent, the two hidden layers can then be easily joined together by the similarity of the bias and weights in them to form a single recurrent layer. The recurrent network helps in memorizing the output from the previous steps. You should always remember that the recurrent network is the unique feature that distinguishes RNNs from other forms of algorithms.

RNNs in AI has been adopted for use in a variety of fields such as:

- **Machine translations** - RNN is applied here to help translate texts or statements from one language to another without altering the original meaning.

- **Speech recognition** - though the input of specific sound waves, RNN is used to predict the phonetic segments which assist in generating words.

- **Generating texts and language modeling** - this follows a sequence of texts introduced in the input layer to predict the next likely word.

- **Image descriptions** - RNN works well here when combined with CNN. The CNN does the segmentation of the image, which is fed into the model at the input layer while the RNN uses the so segmented data to recreate the image descriptions.

Based on the outline concerning RNNs, you can undoubtedly agree that it is designed to function and operate in a way similar to the human brain. This feature makes it easy to apply it in AI for purposes of data and image processing.

Reinforcement Learning (RL)

The main idea behind the reinforcement learning algorithm is learning from interactions with the environment. For instance, assume that during winter, the weather outside is chilly, and your body is freezing, you have to look for some warmth. You then decide to light up fire at the center of your house to keep you warm. Your little sibling then joins you to get some heat too. He approaches the fireplace and feels warm. This makes him understand that fire is a positive thing. The warmth from the fireplace draws him nearer to it, and he eventually decides to touch it but ends up being burned. Ouch! He understands that the fire is not too friendly as he thought. It comes to his understanding that the fire is helpful when you are at a safe distance from it because it gives you warmth, but moving too close to it may get you burned. The same concept of learning applies to RL.

In AI, RL is a type of programming used in training algorithms based on a system of reward and punishment. The software agent here learns through having interactions with the general environment in which he receives awards by taking corrective actions and gets punishments for incorrect responses. In our illustration, the reward is heat or warmth gained by keeping a safe distance from the fireplace while the punishment is getting burned by getting too close to the fire.

Basically, in a simple RL set up, the agent observes his environment, then decides on the best course of action to use in interacting with the existing environment. The result of the actions taken may give the software agent a reward or a punishment. Therefore, in every action taken by the agent, he aims at maximizing his reward.

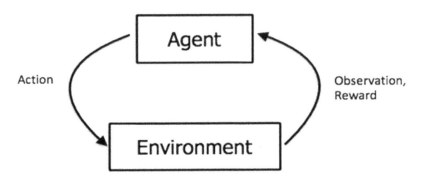

Figure 4: A simple RL setup

The unique feature of RL that makes it stand out among the other types of algorithms is the training of the agents. Here, rather than using the programming data provided, the agent is required to interact with the general environment on its own in an attempt to help it learn ways to maximize rewards while minimizing punishments.

RL has gained popularity in the AI world today following its applications in various fields such as:

- **Medicine** - RL has been applied in the field of medicine to perform clinical trials as well as drug therapies.

- **Gaming** - following the victory of Alpha Go, a machine learning algorithm over a human player in a game, many people have adopted the use of RL in games of all kinds. RL is the algorithms that are mostly used in computer games.

- **Robotics** - owing to the fact that RL can take place without any supervision, it becomes the best option for use in robotics. Its application in the robotics industry has brought with it an exponential growth in robotics.

- **Autonomous vehicles** - RL has been adopted for use in autonomous drones, vehicles, ships, and trucks. The use of reinforcement learning has resulted in considerable growth in the autonomous vehicle industry.

As the position of RL in the AI industry continues to grow, companies will be required to invest more in data and resources to help them understand the various ways in which they can implement this technological advancement in their products, services as well as industrial operations.

Artificial Intelligence and Image Processing

You might be wondering what image processing entails. Image processing refers to the manipulation of an image to extract some information from it or to enhance it. Most images that are taken using regular cameras may be misfocused or even contain lots of noise, and this calls for processing. Image processing may come in the form of edge detection or filtering. From the detailed explanation of AI algorithms, it is evident that there exists a strong link between AI and image processing. Most of the AI algorithms, such as CNNs, RNNs, and RL, are commonly adopted in image processing.

Chapter 6: All in Real Life

With the coming up of Artificial Intelligence, a lot of industries can enhance CX by studying more about customers and forestalling their needs. A lot of CX focused trademarks are arraying Artificial Intelligence technologies tactically at main consumer touchpoints. There are examples of AI-powered CX from various companies that will show customer experience can be an algorithm for accelerative thinking industries.

- **When it comes to retailing, AI personalization unlocks access to 1% customer**

  The information indicates that the top 1% of retailer's buyers are valued 18x further than the average buyer. The best method you can enact for those discerning, high-value buyers is by personalization. Usual personalization such as user-specific page outline is table stake for memorable buyer experience, and thrilling customization is required. This where you will need an advanced machine. Thrilling personalization goes beyond one-off personalized newsletter to a buyer tailored promotions that are distributed at the correct time, to the right device, and with an impeccable message. You can see it as a move from buyer segments to the audience of one.

- **The building of trust and loyalty in a global bank**

  The Royal Bank of Scotland is handling 17 million customers transversely seven trademarks and eight, unlike channels. When you look at its history, their strategy concentrated on aggressive sales goals intending to upsell buyers into current credit cards. From the buyer look of things, this has brought about a heap of digital and paper spam. Royal Bank of Scotland has decided to revamp its partnership with the buyer turning to AI to improve customer experience. The approach was taken to lever data wisdom into entirely new levels of purchaser contact. When a customer severally overdrafts an account, AI flags applicable bank staffs to contact the customer with financial guidance.

- **The specific airline, new data intelligence is driving CX innovation**

  Air Canada is handling 45 million customers yearly, having many people booking online or using a mobile application. They are seeking to improve understand their customers and also enhance the mobile app experience. They have enacted an AI and machine studying info analytics system that gives insight to their customer characteristics through digital and offline frequencies. Company heads leveraged the info analytics vision into customer-facing enactment improvements and streamlined website familiarity.

- **AI battles ticket bots in the entertainment sector**

  The Internet has changed the dynamics of live events by coming up with easily accessible secondary ticket marketplaces like Craigslist and StubHub. Recently automatic bots purchase several tickets, depleting supply, and instantly offer the tickets for sale at main markups. Ticketmaster has changed AI to rewrite rules by the use of a machine learning system known as Verified Fan. This system encourages those buying tickets first to register their interests before tickets go on sale. AI systems analyze each registrant to identify scalper bots behind the scenes. This has resulted in 5% of tickets sold using Verified Fan getting to the secondary marketplaces. Most of the people, more so artists, and fans are so happy with the way of acquiring tickets.

- **Some hotel brand, new insight requires new AI**

To understand customers well, the hospitality industry has enhanced techniques such as mystery shoppers and customer assessments. Leveraging content of many online assessment sites has been seen as difficult or expensive. This was there until the hotel brand Dorchester Collection created a custom AI analytic system that is an essential giant focus group operating endlessly in real-time. The system has been capable of bringing along 75000 guest reviews from 28 hotels transversely 10 trademarks and send its outcomes with a 30-minute film.

AI Changes in Market Place

- **Buying and selling faster regards to AI**

There is a belief that AI can change the way humans shop and are full of joy because of the potential opportunities and worth it's bringing to those buying and selling. AI is improving the marketplace, thus making it more efficient for buyers and giving a more natural interaction between sellers and buyers. AI has automatically enhanced the quality of pictures and translated listings and messenger interactions. There is an introduction of new features that use AI for price range suggestions and automatically categorize. This means that when you want to sell a good, a marketplace can use AI to assist you in selling it quickly by giving options about your price based on comparable amounts of the good. It will also categorize the proper based on the picture and how it is described, making it easier for you. There is an ongoing test on camera features that can use AI to suggest goods you may interest in having, i.e., when you like your friend's shoes, you can have a picture, and marketplace's AI tech can recommend the same product on sale around you.

- **A lot of shopping options within you**

  Adding to the new AI features, there has been an addition of a variety of contents from trades inclusion of vehicles, house rentals, home operations, and shopping from e-commerce dealers. Nowadays, cars are the most vital category for the marketplace worldwide, along with furniture and electronics. After coming up with vehicles on the list of local dealers a year ago, the market has been considered one of the leading destinations for people to acquire and sell already used cars.

- **Building a safe and trusted community**

  Shopping online needs a lot of confidence in the people and trades you are buying from or operating with. This is why you should enhance features that enact a safe and trust community, including:

  - Detect and delete objectionable content: due to AI technology, you can detect and remove items that are violating your policies by analyzing pictures, content, and context.

- Rating buyers and sellers: buyers and sellers can rate each other to know if they have a good or bad experience and leave a comment on what can be improved and its reliability. It also helps people be informed on who to contact, community ratings that assist in the creation of great experiences by enacting good character.

- A lot of Robust reporting tools: the community has helped to make buying and selling better for anyone by giving content that doesn't go along with the marketplace. You can report the listing of items that are violating commerce policies. You can also inform buyers and sellers doing illegal activities.

Just Getting Started

When you look back the past two years, you will be inspired by the people across the world using the marketplace to do great activities. There are stories like that of Rudolph and his family who bonded with his family and community after the loss of his wife through cancer by selling birdhouses for a cause. They have continued to work on delivering new useful features that you have an interest in.

AI Changes in Time Management

Most of us are not capable of working on everything we planned to execute in the morning. It's on rare occasions when someone can perform all the plans on the list. This will pile up the tasks daily and weekly. This is a point where time management will be changed to time intelligence when connected to artificial intelligence. You can employ AI to assist in the cumbersome lifting process of putting together data and context. This will give it a centralized system.

Automated Information Harvesting

AI technology permits automated info harvesting to have a business plan. There is control of manual time inputs from the workers; thus, it automatically collects data from the trade ecosystem, holding it back to particular deliverables and the limitations. It provides you with facial identification technology where a worker can walk to their time clock and log in by the use of facial identification. Due to this, the process tends to be faster, accessible, and gives advantages of biometrics without any added course or software costs.

Receiving Assistance from Personal Assistants

This is one of the most familiar kinds of AI that you have come across. Alexa, Google Now, and Siri are usual AI-powered systems that can study your demands and characteristics. They will provide you with essential data when asked a question. Other AI manufacturers keep their focus on creating a wise to-do-list that can assist you in prioritizing your tasks and sending notices. They can give a record of how they have been performing previously. Others can also help you plan your emails, alert you about traveling, manage your contact lists and pictures.

Manage Task in Real-Time

With info becoming real-time, trades have sorted to make crucial decisions immediately. Heads-Suite and managers can have advance notices and alerts that cause them to have a pro-active approach while making verdicts.

Customizing Workflow

A lot of trades are having problems when it comes to timesheets, the trouble of exceptions, mistakes, and unpredictability. Wise workflows simplify the trade processes by validating the real-time data with built-in exemption; thus, an admin can see where and when it brings a positive impact.

Artificial Intelligence-powered time management tools work in different ways, like:

- **Habit** – AI-enabled tool will note down your habits and give suggestions on due dates, preferably. In case you reply to your mails on Monday morning, then the due response can be set for that particular day.

- **Task priority** – the tool can estimate the urgency of any kind of task by tracking the information unknowingly from the to-do list.

- **Keeping a record of weekdays and weekends** – the tool can store files of duties that you can execute on weekdays. It will also schedule tasks to be done weekly.

- **Upcoming tasks** – if you are full of tasks on a Thursday and you are free on Friday, then AI will try to balance the load throughout the seven days appropriately.

- **Daily and weekly visions** – you can plan your daily and weekly perceptions depending on the tasks you want to execute daily and weekly. The time management tool can assist the due dates, thus helping you meet explicit goals.

You find yourself able to define business goals and create a data model to enhance and give feedback; then, you can use AI for resource optimization and preparation. This can help transport and have logistics in your trade. Forecasting is the best method you can employ to help exceptional tuning project execution and reduce the number of misses. When you decide to use Artificial Intelligence in improving your project enactment, you need to get ways to try and enhance. Most of the AI-powered tools are capable of learning from habits by the use of artificial intelligence, suggesting any necessary changes.

AI Handling Customer Retention and Interaction

Most of the successful marketing sections should ask themselves questions about what their customers want and what kind of goods will suit and meet the wants of a customer. They can answer such questions by the use of artificial intelligence.

Improvement of Human-Computer Interactions

Natural language processing and machine learning are capable projects around the vast area of AI that can be used to enhance and improve the product to be discovered and overall buying experience. Speech identification, along with national language understanding, among others, is capable of options that will allow people to use spoken or scripted sentences to communicate with computer systems. This will enable customers to interact requests directly, unlike going through other interfaces on a device like a mobile phone, table, among others. NLP changes the spoken word to have the intent of the user and when used in partnership with the user's context, can make it to like its more than artificial. Cognitive methods, like deep learning, can increase the process. Advance supervised and unsupervised ML methods can be put in use to enhance advanced models and algorithms. Due to this, commerce systems improved by ML, and AI will wisely cross-sell and up-sell compelling proposals. This will bring about an increase in conversation rates, general order worth, and buyer loyalty and buyer lifetime value.

Assists in Identifying the Needs of a Customer

A lot of many marketers are taking advantage of massive data and predictive analysis for presentation. The logic that the larger the information sets and there is an increase of powerful algorithms being used thus high commendations from customers. Personalized engines will put together personal character with microdata tracking their characteristics along with touchpoint trademarks to make a decision about products and services based on previous needs. This gathers customer data with internet information basing on ML analysis that will incorporate things such as time spent when requesting, clicks, scrolls, and interest levels. When many people are using the Internet and purchasing utilizing the trademark, then there will be better and easy personalization. Buyers will be free to provide insights to personal interests and considering the purchase of the systems.

Improves Your Pricing and Makes It Dynamic

The biggest problem faced by pricing managers is the daily fluctuation. E-commerce companies have platforms that assist in the management of supply and demand with ML that can partition customer buyer segments. This will provide the trade with the power to pinpoint the cost of customers who can pay at a personal level. It also examines customer data and confirms the price a customer is able to pay. Overlooked benefits of AI changes the story in e-commerce and service operation. AI unlocks the hidden pattern in programmer characteristics to learn or study the steps to make or the best opportunities for success. When you are leveraging NLP, the buyer will also get experience, and trade gains profitable insight. This will bring a win for the customer and the brand.

AI Application in Common Life

- **Medical and Chemical Research**
  - **Medical imaging**- medical scans are systematically gathered and kept for some time until they are available to train AI systems. AI cuts the cost and time in scans, thus giving the advantage to have better treatment. AI is providing results that are encouraging to detect pneumonia, cancer, and eye diseases.
  - **Surgery** – robots that are controlled by AI are being used to handle specific tasks during surgery, such as tying knots to close wounds.

- **Sex Industry**

  Testing a dataset that is the same as the training dataset containing silhouettes shaping people to copy real images in human trafficking cases that victims use a black overlay. Systems have been trained to identify hotel-based rooms décor. Most of the top pictures retracted are from the right hotel chain.

- **Transportation Industry**

  It will ensure safety for all road users: the safety of passengers, pedestrians, and drivers is one of the biggest concerns in the transportation industry. AI has decreased the number of human errors. It has been able to predict and monitor traffic. Prediction ways will assist you in performing traffic conditions and automatically calculating alternative methods. There will be vehicle maintenance that predicts using intelligent sensors and dashboards. There will be an implementation of driver characteristics that check and enhances safety and increase production. It can analyze sensor information and check your fleet through data-driven dashboards for wise trains, ships, and trucks connectivity. AI can adjust your route to avoid congestion and incidents and allocate time for occasions where jams are unavoidable.

- **Teaching Industry**

AI has brought about a high impact in the teaching industry by simplifying administrative duties. It has an automated expedition of administrative tasks for teachers and institutions. AI has come up with great ways of grading systems and has gained a lot in the school admissions board. Smart content will be there to give students techniques in achieving academic success. AI technology has technology that has been utilized in students, and they are being taught in schools. AI tutoring systems can give natural feedback and work with students directly. The methods are inception and can become digital teachers and assist students with educational wants. AI enacts global learning because education has no limits, thus AI eliminating boundaries. AI has enhanced IT processes unleashing new efficiencies.

- **Agriculture Industry**

Agriculture and farming is a very vital important profession worldwide. AI has helped in analyzing farm information. Farms give lots of thousands of details on the ground every day. AI has assisted farmers in analyzing a range of things in concurrent like meteorological conditions, high-temperature usage of water from their farmstead to augment enhanced pronouncements. AI expertise assists agriculturalists to have plans to create a lot of yields by determining the type of choices, hybrid seed options, and resourceful utilization. Agriculturalists are exhausting AI to mend recurrent models, thus improving precision in agriculture and increase production. The models can predict weather patterns months and help farmers to make decisions. Seasonal forecasting is valuable for small scale farmers as it helps in improving the countries as their information can be restricted.

Possession of the small ranches to carry on working and developing yields are vital because they help in the production of 70% of the world's crops. AI tackles labor challenges, and this is because of the workforce challenge. Most farms need many laborers to help harvest crops and keep the farms productive. A solution for assisting the shortage of workers AI agriculture bots. The bots have been used in augment of human labor using different forms. The bots can do harvesting at higher volume and quicker speed than social workers. The bots do work accurately by identifying and eliminating weeds. They have reduced the costs of farms by working all through, unlike the human workforce.

AI Changes in Bank System for a Customer

Banks have a hard time trying to reduce costs, meet margins, and exceed customer expectations through individual experience. To enhance this, the implementation of AI is very vital. Most banks have begun embracing AI and connected technologies worldwide. A study by the National Business Research Institute, states that 32% of financial organizations are using AI by the use of voice recognition and predicting analysis. Coming up with mobile technology has a large playing field in the banking sector. Automated AI-powered customer service has gained a firm grip. AI features have enabled services, offers, and insights within programmers' characteristics and necessities. Cognitive machines have been trained to advise and interact by giving an analysis of programmers' data. A lot of banks are deploying tools to help in examining transactions in real-time.

Examples of Artificial Intelligence

Email Spam Filters

The filters are using machine learning, forming AI to learn which emails you want and don't. That is not the only AI you can have in your inbox. Google has come up with an AI-powered service known as Smart Reply that has created a short email message that has helped to reply suggestions basing on the respondent to familiar messages.

Collaboration Tool Slack

Slack is a chat tool that is being used by trade organizations for putting together communication. A lot of organizations have never realized that slack is using AI behind the scenes to help in analyzing of information it has gathered about every company and its workers using the tool. This is, therefore, enhancing developments and improving the production of people using it.

Teslas Studying from Other Teslas

Tesla cars have connected and learned from one another, even though Elon Musk has ruffled feathers in the AI world. In any case, a vehicle moves to avoid hurdles on the highway; the other fleet will get to know what to do after the updates are delivered, sharing information. The team is still working to build full automatically cars for your road, and AI is part of their operation.

Video Games

Artificial intelligence has been associated with a video game for a very long time, and now more of its applications are sophisticated. When it comes to game series, AI individuals have revolved basing on their communication with players. Nowadays, all the video games played are empowered by AI in some way.

Music Compositions

When you want help to focus, relax, meditate, or sleep, you might try out Brain.fm, this is the most advanced AI music writer in the world. Most of the music in the service is created by AI and has been tested for its results to create music. The brain craves to achieve the desired outcome, and this is not the only way AI is making steps in the airwaves.

Self-Driving Cars

One of the significant applications AI innovated autonomous vehicles. The idea was earlier on a sci-fi fantasy, and it's now a practical reality. Most people were skeptical about the technology when it was starting, driverless cars have already been introduced in the transportation industry. Automated taxis have already begun to be operational in Tokyo. For safety measures, a driver is supposed to sit in the car to control the vehicle in case of an emergency. The founder of the cars has said that the technology will help in reducing the cost of taxi operations thus will help increase public transportation modes in remote regions.

American logistics have embraced automatic trucks to harvest a lot of benefits. With the coming of autonomous trucks, maintenance and administration values will reduce by 45%. The majority of companies are still working on their pilot projects, thus striving to enhance self-driving vehicles flawless and safe for passengers. This technology has evolved, and self-driven cars have already gained high confidence and have been mainstream in the consumer realm. The vehicle has a combination of different sensors to perceive its surroundings; such sensors include radar, sonar, and inertial measurement units.

Chapter 7: Data Science

Data science is an interdisciplinary mix of data logic, algorithm development, and technology to unravel scientifically difficult issues. At its core is a collection of raw data, streaming in and stored in company data warehouses. Data science is a discipline that unifies statistics, information analysis, machine learning, and their common methods to understand and analyze real occurrences with data. Data science employs techniques and approaches drawn from several fields in the context of arithmetic, statistics, engineering science, and data science. Data science is alluded to be a "fourth paradigm" of science (empirical, theoretical, process, and currently information-driven). The entirety of science is dynamic due to the impact of information technology, therefore, causing the data flood.

Data science is about using this discovered data in creative ways to get value for your business. We can build advanced capabilities with it. We can learn and build advanced potentiality from the data that we mine.

Data science is an umbrella term that encompasses information analytics, data mining, machine learning, and several other connected disciplines. Whereas a data scientist is anticipated to forecast the future supported by past patterns, information analysts extract meaty insights from varied information sources. A data scientist creates queries, whereas a data analyst finds answers to the present set of queries.

Data Mining, Analysis, and Insight

Data analysis and data mining belong to the business intelligence (BI) subset that additionally integrates data warehousing, online analytical processing (OLAP), and database management systems. Data analytics likewise encompasses a couple of completely different branches of broader statistics and analysis that facilitates combining various sources of data and find connections, therefore, simplifying the results.

These facets of data science are each regarding discovering findings from data. Plunging in at a crude level to mine, observe and understand complicated trends, behaviors, and assumptions. It is about regression analysis of buried insight, which will facilitate corporations to form smarter business decisions.

You have four V's that are used regarding big data; volume, veracity, velocity, and variety. Another V exists that is vital for your knowledge- validity. There is a proverb in programming– "Garbage in, garbage out." the standard of your analysis depends on the standard of your data.

The collection of data might constitute conducting surveys, polls, or doing different experiments. Throughout this collection, data might increasingly become contaminated, which can yield incorrect analysis or contribute to creating the wrong business decisions. While ways of research could contradict by subject area, the optimum stage for deciding applicable scientific procedures happens at the beginning of the analysis method and should not be a second thought.

The increasing data being generated annually maintain obtaining useful information that is a lot more vital. The data often is kept in a data warehouse, summarized data from internal systems, and data from external sources, a repository of information gathered from varied sources, together with company databases. Analysis of the report includes simple query databases and recording, applied math analysis, data mining, and a lot of complex inter-dimensional analysis.

As an example:

- Netflix mines data on movie watching patterns to know what drives client interest and applies that data to form selections on that Netflix original series to introduce.
- Target identifies the customers' distinctive shopping behaviors among their major customer segments that help to guide electronic communication to an entirely diverse market.
- Proctor & Gamble utilizes statistical designs to clearly perceive prospective demand, which facilitates set up for production levels more successfully.

How do data scientists excavate insights? They begin with data research. When presented with a difficult query, data scientists become investigators. They investigate the evidence and attempt to decipher patterns or characteristics among the data. This skill needs some analytical ability. Then, information scientists apply the quantitative technique to understand the information at a more profound level- for instance, segmentation analysis, presumed models, statistical forecasting, artificial control experiments, etc. The intent is to scientifically put together a forensic overview of exactly what the data is admittedly putting across. Data-driven insight is pivotal to providing clever, calculated steerage. Therefore, data scientists assume the role of consultants, offering insight to business stakeholders on how to work on the findings.

The purpose of collecting company data jointly in one structure- generally in a company's data warehouse- is to expedite analysis, so data that is collected from a range of various company activities are applied to enhance the understanding of fundamental trends in their business. One of the fastest- growing areas in data science is most frequently related to multidimensional analysis.

An effective data repositioning strategy needs a robust, nimble, and straightforward way to cultivate advantageous information from collected data. Data mining tools and analysis use quantitative methods, pattern recognition, correlation finding, cluster analysis, and associations to research data with minimal or no IT interference. The ensuing information is then given to the customer in a comprehensive form. The processes are jointly referred to as business intelligence. Managers will choose from many kinds of analysis tools, together with reports and queries, managed query environments, and OLAP and its alternatives. These are supported by data mining that develops patterns that will be applied for subsequent analysis completing the BI method.

Data Types

Data types are a crucial statistics concept that must be understood to exploit statistical analysis to your data correctly and to draw accurate inferences regarding the data adequately. The first factor to try to do after you begin learning statistics is becoming aware of the data variables that are used, like numerical and categorical variables. Differing variables need differing kinds of applied math and visualization approaches.

Having a decent knowledge of the various data variables, also known as measurement scales, could be a fundamental requirement for performing Exploratory Data Analysis (EDA) because you can only apply specific statistical measurements for particular data types. You further ought to understand the data variable that you will apply to settle on the correct visualization technique. Data types should be considered as the simplest way of classifying different variables. Two main types of variables or measurement scales are:

Numerical

Numerical data is measurable information, and it is, of course, data described as numbers and not words or text. Like a person's weight, height, blood pressure, or IQ. Or perhaps the data is a count, like a number of stock shares owned by an individual, the number of chapters in a literary piece, or how many books you will be able to read of your favorite author before the end of the year. (Statistic experts conjointly refer to numerical data as quantitative data.)

Nominal data are often additionally split into two types: distinct and continuous. Note that nominal data that has no order; so, if you would alter the arrangement of its values, then the effect would remain unaltered.

Discrete Data

Discrete data has a logical conclusion to it. It represents things that may be counted; it makes out probable values that may be recorded. The list of actual values could also be finite (also referred to as fixed), or it is going to start from 0, 1, 2, on to eternity (making it computationally infinite). As an illustration, the quantity of tails in one hundred coin tosses assumes values from zero through the finite case to one hundred. However, the number of tosses required to arrive at one hundred tails assumes values from one hundred onwards to eternity (if you never arrive at the one-hundredth tails). The possible values of the coin toss are then listed as one hundred, 101, 102, 103, and so on (representing the countably infinite case).

Continuous data

Continuous data does not have a logical end to it. It represents measurements; its possible values cannot be counted and might solely be delineated with intervals on the real number line. To illustrate, the precise quantity of liquid petroleum bought at the pump for cars with 30-liter tanks would be continuous data from zero liters to thirty liters, described by the 0 to30 intervals inclusive. You may pump 10.20 liters, or 10.21, or 10.214863 liters, or any amount from zero to thirty. Using this approach, continuous data is often considered as computationally infinite. For simple record keeping, data analysts sometimes select out one number within the range to round off.

When you are collecting numerical data, you use:

- Frequencies: A frequency is a rate that one thing happens over an amount of time or at intervals in a dataset.
- Proportion: The proportion is calculated by dividing the frequency by the overall sum of events.
- Percentage.

Visualization Methods: to examine nominal information, you will be able to use a bar chart or a pie chart.

Categorical

Categorical data is often any data that is not a number, which might mean a string of text or date. These variables may be softened into nominal and ordinal values, although you would not typically see this done. Categorical data represents characteristics. So, it will represent things like a person's language, ethnicity, etc. Categorical data may also defy numerical values (Taking an example: 1 for "on" and 0 for "off"). It is important to note that these numbers do not have any meaning in the mathematical sense.

Ordinal

Ordinal values describe discretely and ordered units. Examples of ordinal values include having a priority on a virus as "Critical" or "Low" or the ranking of a restaurant as "Five Star" or "Three Star." Therefore, it is possible to encapsulate your ordinal information with frequencies, proportions, and percentages. By doing this, you will be able to visualize the data through a bar or pie chart. Besides, you will be able to use median, percentiles, mode, and also the interquartile range to compile your data.

In addition to ordinal and nominal values, there is a select sort of categorical data known as binary. Binary data types solely have two values – yes or no. They could be described in numerous ways like "True" and "False" or one and zero. Binary data is employed heavily for classification machine learning models. Samples of binary variables will include whether or not an individual has stopped their subscription service or not, or if an individual bought a car or not.

Clustering

The purpose of classification and clustering algorithms is to make sense of and extract worth from giant sets of both unstructured and structured data. When you are operating with vast volumes of disorganized data, you would be smart to partition the data into some logical groupings before trying to analyze it. A loose definition of a cluster can be the method of organizing items into groups that have members with similar characteristics.

Clustering and classification allow you to look broadly at your data en bloc, to create some logical structures supported by what you discover there before delving deeper into the practical analysis.

Clusters, in their purest form, are sets of data points that share similar characteristics, and cluster algorithms are the ways that classify these points of data into totally distinguished clusters grounded by their correlation. You will see cluster algorithms applied for disease classification in medical sciences. You will also know the algorithm applied for client classification in research and environmental engineering and health risk assessment.

There are two different clustering ways, depending on your dataset:

- **Hierarchical**: Algorithms produce individual sets of nested clusters, every in their own rank level.

- **Partitional**: Algorithms produce only one set of clusters.

Clustering may be thought of as the most significant unsupervised learning hurdle; thus, like every alternative drawback of this sort, clustering deals with finding a system in an exceeding compilation of unlabeled data.

Importance of Clustering

The goal of clustering is to work out the inherent grouping in a collection of unstructured data. However, do we decide what consists of a decent cluster? It may be shown that there is no perfect "ideal" criterion, which might be free of the ultimate goal of clustering. As a result, it is the user that should provide this criterion in a manner that the outcome of the cluster suits their desires.

Take, for instance. People tend to be interested in finding representatives for homogenized teams, in finding "natural clusters" and describe their anonymous properties ("natural" data types), to find advantageous and suitable groupings or to find uncommon data pieces.

Clustering Applications

Clustering algorithms may be applied in several industries, for instance:

- Marketing: to find groups of shoppers with similar behavior given an extensive customer information database containing their features and historic shopping records.
- City-planning: characterizing groups of homes per the type of house, price, and geographical location.
- Biology: using taxonomy, the classification of animals and plants is given their features.
- Libraries: checking books;
- Insurance: distinguishing groups of motor contract holders with a higher average claim cost; as well as identifying fraud;
- Earthquake studies: determine earthquake epicenters to spot dangerous zones;

The primary necessities that a clustering algorithmic rule ought to satisfy are:

1. Scalability
2. Ability to deal with differing kinds of attributes
3. High dimensionality
4. Discovering clusters with discretionary form;
5. Interpretability and value
6. Minimal needs for domain information to work out input criterion;
7. Capacity to handle noise and unusual data objects
8. Insensitivity to the arrangement of input records

Clustering Limitations

There are a few issues with clustering, among which include:

- Current cluster techniques do not cater to all the requirements sufficiently (and simultaneously)
- Big data and dealing with a wide range of dimensions may be problematic due to time complexity
- The results of the classification algorithm (which in several cases may be discretionary itself) may be taken in numerous ways.
- The effectiveness of the cluster strategy depends on the description of "distance" (as in distance-based clustering), but if a physical distance does not exist, we have a tendency to "define" it, which is not an easy task, particularly in multidimensional spaces

Applications of data science include:

Internet search engines use data science algorithms to deliver the matching results for search queries in a fraction of a second.

Digital Advertisements, including the complete digital marketing spectrum, uses the data science algorithms- from show banners to digital billboards. This is often the main reason for digital adverts obtaining a higher click-through rate than traditional advertisements.

Recommender systems do not merely make it simple to seek out relevant products from billions of products on the market yet also adds loads to user-experience. Many firms use this technique to market their products and suggestions per the user's demands and connection of data. The recommendations are supported by the user's previous search results.

Watson, by IBM, is an AI technology that helps physicians quickly determine critical data in a patient's medical history to gather relevant evidence and explore treatment choices. Watson collects a patient's medical records then provides its evident-based and personalized recommendation powered by data from a curated assortment of journals, textbooks, and pages of texts that offer doctors instant access to an abundance of information customized to the patient's treatment plan.

Blueberry is an example of a robot created by Kory Mathewson, that can perform improv comedy as a result of being fed subtitles from many thousands of films. He trained it to make lines of dialogue for an improv performance by rewarding it once the dialogue was sensible and punishing it once it spoke nonsense. While Blueberry will not be auditioning at a talent show in the near future, this lovely robot will often hit the proper notes with funny lines.

Chapter 8: Internet of Things

One of the most common concepts today in the mobile app development world is the Internet of Things. From the simplest consumer applications such as wearables and smart homes to the most complex industry solutions like driverless forklifts, the Internet of Things (IoT) has penetrated every aspect of technology and is gradually changing the way that we live, interact with others, and work with internet-enabled devices.

In a report recently published by Statista, more than 31 billion devices, including smartphones, cars, smartwatches, and wearable, will be connected by the end of 2020. The number is currently recorded at 23 billion, which is a demonstration of the exponential growth of IoT.

While the concept of IoT has been in the public realm for a very long time, many people are still not familiar with it or how it functions. In this chapter, we are going to understand the key concept as well as its application.

What is the Internet of Things (IoT)?

The Internet of Things (IoT) simply refers to the connected ecosystem of physical devices, appliances, vehicles, and other things that can collect data and exchange it through a wireless and wired network without any human-to-computer or human-to-human intervention. Through the enables integration and exchange of data by the physical devices, this technology focuses on enhancing people's lives through the provision of comfort and simplicity with possible efficiency.

Through the integration of complex technologies such as Artificial Intelligence (AI), machine learning, and machine-to-machine communication, IoT aims towards extending the connectivity of physical things beyond the common internet-supported devices such as tablets, PCs, and smartphones to a wider spectrum of non-internet enabled objects like coffee makers, door locks, and washing machines. This approach is important as it will enable humans to control and monitor them with the help of a simple mobile gadget.

How IoT Works

Just as other computer devices and systems have predefined components and steps, so does the Internet of Things. A complete IoT system constitutes four components that work together to ensure the system provides a desirable outcome. The key components are discussed below.

- **Sensors/Devices**

  Sensors or devices collect even the minutest data from the surrounding environment, which could include simple information as geographical location or complex data like the health history of a patient. In order to pick up this form of data, multiple sensors can be bundled together to form a device that is able to perform complex tasks than a simple sensing activity. For example, a smartphone is composed of several in-built sensors like Camera, GPS, and Accelerometer, without which could hinder the phone from sensing any data.

Thus, the first step to the functioning of IoT is the collection of minute data from the surrounding environment through the use of multiple sensors.

- **Connectivity**

After data has been collected by sensors or devices, it goes to the cloud infrastructure, which is the IoT platform through the use of a medium. Here, there are several wired and wireless networking technologies like Wi-Fi, Bluetooth, LPQAN, Cellular Networks, and Ethernet that transmit the collected data. Although the connectivity options represent the interaction of connection range, power consumption, and bandwidth, choosing the one that transmits data to the cloud significantly depends on the specific requirements and the complexity levels of the IoT application.

- **Processing of data**

After data has been transmitted to the clouds, it is stored, processed, and analyzed through the use of Big Data Analytics Engine to enhance decision making. The analysis process can be as simple as checking the temperature of an AC, or as complex as identifying burglars into a house through the use of surveillance cameras. Once the data is processed, it is used to conduct immediate action that can turn an ordinary physical device into a smart one.

- **The user interface**

  In this last step, the IoT system notifies the consumer about the action through text, email, alert, or notification sound that is triggered by the system. The user can then either leave the notified action intact, manually perform an action that affects the system, or proactively check the IoT system. For example, if a user realizes some changes in a particular room, he/she could adjust the room temperature using the IoT app that is installed on his/her device.

Benefits of IoT

Although the main goal of IoT is to automate human life and make everything efficient, there are several other benefits that the technology offer to consumers and businesses. Some of the key benefits include:

- **Easy access to data**

  Everyone, including entrepreneurs and marketers, love quality data, and with the invention of IoT, firms are able to effectively access data that relate to their consumers and products more than ever. They are able to take advantage of the real-time operation insights they obtain from IoT devices to monitor the behaviors of their customers, enhance the consumer experience, and make smarter decisions. Simply put, the more information you have, the more you are likely to make the right choices.

- **Better tracking and management**

  With IoT, industries are able to track, and management has become very easy. From monitoring road traffic and weather changes and tracking inventories to notifying authorities of any illegal or worrying activities, IoT has revolutionized the way that people manage and track their business assets. IoT system is not just about smart devices or smart homes; it is now a smart office, a smart service, and smart everything.

- **Efficient utilization of resources**

Whether it is home, hotel, office, or car, the Internet of Things facilitates the efficient utilization of assets with the aim of improving productivity. Through the advantage of interactions of machines, an IoT system is able to gather real-time data through the use of actuators and sensors in order to further use the big data to improve efficiency while also minimizing human intervention. An example is when your home appliance alerts you of a completed task, you will never worry about the efficient use of power at your home.

- **Automation and control**

IoT promotes automation since the devices are always connected to each other via a wireless network, which makes them operate on their own without excess intervention. For example, your home appliances like washing machines, air conditioners, and an oven can operate automatically even without your monitoring or controlling them remotely.

- **Enhances comfort and convenience**

We are living in a society that is fast-paced, and people are very busy that they don't care about little things such as reading power meters or switching off lights. However, with IoT, such problems can be addressed since the interconnectivity of data and devices offer full control over devices that are connected to the IoT system. With your ability to control your home devices through a centralized device such as a smartphone, you can enhance convenience and comfort.

- **Saves time and money**

  The use of IoT involves getting more done with as little effort as possible through automated tasks and little human intervention. Being able to accomplish your cumbersome tasks faster without the use of energy, IoT enables you to save your hard-earned money and save your quality time. For instance, if one of the electronic appliances is able to turn itself off after a task, you will save the effort and time you may have required to witch the appliance of manually.

Use Cases of Internet of Things

Some of the real-world applications of IoT are:

- **Smart Home**

  A smart home remains the best example of IoT technology. Smart home devices and systems offer optimum security and convenience to users and are designed to save energy and time. With a smart home, you can control everything in your home, from temperature to lighting with just a simple smartphone control.

- **Wearables**

  Although there are wide varieties of smartwatches and fitness tracking devices in the market, many superpowers like Intel and Samsung have begun investing in IoT-powered wearables. Through the use of installed software and sensors, these devices are able to track and monitor significant health metrics like eating habits, blood pressure, sleeping habits, heart rates, and caloric intake.

- **Smart cities**

Different countries, including the UK, Spain, Japan, and South Korea, are making efforts to colonize smart cities with the aim of providing their citizens with the best and healthier environment to live in. The countries collect data from assets, citizens, and devices with the aim of solving major challenges that people in those cities face like crime, congestion, water distribution, and waste management.

- **Automotive and transportation**

With IoT, companies in the automotive industry like Tesla, Ford, Volvo, and BMW are already planning to enhance their in-car experience. With advanced technologies such as computer vision, sensors, sonar, internet, and maps, these vehicles operate without drivers and can run without any human assistance. If combined with machine learning, IoT in the transport sector can help to perform roles like smart traffic control, smart parking, fleet management, and logistics.

- **Medical and Healthcare**

The field of medicine is currently utilizing IoT powered devices to offer remote emergency alerts and health monitoring services. Through the use of smart healthcare devices, doctors are able to monitor their patients' health away from the clinical environment and provide medicine on the basis of relevant data. Also, doctors in the emergency department keep themselves ready for any emergencies because IoT enables them to be aware of their patients' medical conditions.

- **Industrial IoT**

  Industrial IoT is the subfield of IoT that leverages the technology used to solve industrial problems, eliminate efficiencies, and automate industrial processes. Apart from the manufacturing industry, other applications of industrial IoT include aerospace, energy management, defense, and futuristic farming.

Internet of Everything and its Relation to IoT

The concept of the Internet of Everything (IoE) is based on the ideology of all-rounded intelligence, connectivity, and cognition. The concept refers to the intelligent internet connections that are not restricted by any devices such as smartphones, computers, and tablets. IoE encompasses any object with digital features that is able to connect to the network of other objects, processes, or people to generate and exchange information as well as facilitate decision-making.

The philosophy of IoE depicts a society where billions of sensors are implanted in different machines, devices, and ordinary objects in order to expand their networking opportunities, thus enhancing their ability to be smart. The key features of IoE include:

- **Decentralization**—With IoE, data is processed in several distributed nodes rather than in a single center.

- **Data input and output**—IoE enables external data to be put into devices and shared with other network components

- **Relates to all digital transformation processes**— IoE technology is interconnected with several digital processes, including AI, Big Data, machine learning, fog computing, and cloud computing.

Elements of IoE

There are four constituent elements of IoE, which include:

- **People**— People offer personal insights through applications, websites, and connected devices that they use. This data is usually analyzed by smart technologies and AI algorithms in order to understand the issues affecting humans and provide relevant content in line with personal needs. This helps to provide quicker solutions necessary for making decisions.

- **Things**— These are the pure concepts of IoE. Several physical items that are embedded with actuators and sensors help generate data about their status and send them to specified destinations across the IoE network.

- **Data**— Raw data that is generated by devices does not have any value. However, once it is summarized and analyzed, it becomes so priceless that it can empower several systems and intelligent solutions.

- **Processes**—Different processes involved in IoE ensure that the correct information is received at the right time and sent to the right person. The goal of IoE processes is to ensure the best usage of Big Data.

The Relationship Between IoT and IoE

The Internet of Things is not the same as IoE. The core difference between the two lies in the number of pillars that each concept has:

- IoE relies on four components, which include things, people, data, and processes

- IoT only focuses on physical objects

In essence, IoT involves the interconnectivity of objects that send and receive information while IoE is a term that widely includes several technologies and people as the receiving end.

Although the two concepts differ, they have common similarities:

- **Decentralization**— Both IoE and IoT are distributed and lack central points; each of them work as a small management center focused on performing certain tasks independently from human intervention.

- **Security issues**— The systems are still very vulnerable to cyberattacks and penetration; with more connection of devices, they become more susceptible to breaches.

How AI and IoT Can Be Combined for More Success and Reliability

While IoT collects data from the surrounding environment, the AI acts as the master "brain" that analyzes the data to aid in decision making. This means that IoT collects data while AI activities process this data and provide its meaning. The useful integration of the two technologies is more apparent in the current systems used by sport tracking devices such as Siri, Alexa, and Google Home.

With connected devices, thanks to IoT, more data can be collected to offer incredible knowledge for companies and the general public. However, this data cannot be helpful to anyone if it is not analyzed. And this is where AI comes into play, utilizing the huge amounts of data to predict trends and offer solutions. Thus, technology developers must improve the integration of AI with IoT data through the following:

IoT and AI Data Analysis

AI relies on four different IoT data analyses, which include:

- Streaming data visualization— In order to integrate IoT with AI, developers must treat streaming data by displaying, defining, and discovering the collected data using intelligent ways to enhance decision-making.

- Accuracy of data time series—It is necessary to maintain a high confidence level of data that has been collected to enhance the integrity

- Advanced and predictive analysis—It is very important to analyze data collected using advanced and predictive techniques.

- Maintain the flow of geospatial and real-time data.

AI in IoT Applications

Visual microdata gathered by IoT can only be understood with AI applications, which would be able to interpret the context of the images. New sensors will also enable computers to collect data through audio formats within the user's environment.

Chapter 9: Artificial Intelligence Superpowers

The United States has protracted its stay as a frontrunner in synthetic intelligence. But conferring to Dr. Kai Fu Lee-one of the sphere's utmost cherished whizzes on AI, China has at present trapped up with the United States at an astonishingly fast stride. As the rivalry between the two countries rises, Lee is foreseeing the two countries, China and the United States, bring into being a foremost duopoly in AI. The Chinese and American administrations will have to familiarize themselves with the fluctuating commercial scenery as a result of AI disruptions.

China and the United States, by this time, have a prime above other nations in artificial intelligence engineering. Even though you will realize improvements and innovations from other nations such as the United Kingdom, France, Singapore, Canada, these countries are dedicating a lot of resources in the event of AI. They have already established active AI inquiry labs manned with abundant ability, but they a shortage in the venture -investment ecological unit and enormous employer stations to produce the Statistics that will be key to the era of putting into practice that you find in the United States and China.

As AI establishments in the United States and China gather supplementary statistics and endowment, the honorable sphere of data-driven progress in broadening their tip to a point somewhere its backbone convert firm for the other countries to launch any meaningful challenge. China and the United States are at this time nurturing the AI monsters that will take over worldwide markets and excerpt treasure from clients everywhere in the earth.

Lee explains that China has precipitously gathered up to the United States at a surprisingly fast and unpredicted, and as a result of this competition, he argues, dramatic changes may happen sooner than you expected.

Supreme whizzes have, by this time, foreseen that AI will have an upsetting influence on blue color occupations. The experts have urged the two nations to agree to take and encircle the abundant accountabilities that emanate with substantial technical power. Lee argues that it is not only the blue-collar jobs that will be affected. He believes the technological advancement will have an impact on white-collar jobs as well. Lee goes ahead to provide a perfect depiction of the tasks which will be exaggerated and how rapid. He gives his suggestion on the resolutions to some of the philosophical deviations in times gone by that are upcoming quickly.

Who Will Triumph the AI Competition Between the US and China?

Currently, in internet AI, Chinese and American corporations are on equivalent footing. However, it is, however, foreseen that Chinese machinery syndicates will have a minor improvement over their American counterparts in the next five years to come.

In business AI, the states are leading the pack. However, China is expected to close in fast in the next five years. It is likely that China will hold up behind in the commercial world, but it is likely to tip in unrestricted facilities and businesses with the prospective to swell in advance on old-fashioned schemes.

Awareness AI is also outcoming its manner into our day-to-day subsists. It is digitizing your bodily biosphere, erudition to be familiar with appearances, appreciates applications, and has graphics of the biosphere around us. The Chinese culture has little concern about statistics disclosure will provide a positive edge in the carrying out. So, consequently, at this time, China's is slightly ahead of the states in perception AI but is expected to open a wide range and lead the rules and the rest of the biosphere in discernment AI in the next five years.

In Autonomous AI currently, the United States is leading the rest of the world in self-driving cars, but as advancement in autonomous technology continues to be realized, China is expected to level the completion with the United States in the next five years. China already has the authority in hardware concentrated solicitations such as self-governing drones.

Is China the Succeeding Global force?

China's general attention on AI and the possessions it is conveying to the struggle could let it take the lead in the field of AI, according to AI experts. The United States has long been perceived as the universal spearhead in modernization, which comprises the field of artificial brainpower. China has extensively been regarded as a technical impersonator. This, nevertheless, has changed drastically and may not be the same anymore. According to the experts, China is poised to take the lead in the coming few years. China's favorable policies on AI, its enormous group of statistics, and the gigantic marketplace, as well as the existence of painstaking and go-getting industrialists, could support the nation overhaul the United States in Artificial intelligence.

However, it is essential to note that the two countries are parallel universes, and each is making its own progress in the world of AI. The United States is a quiet way forward in the primary expertise from the inquiry test center and campuses. But China is nowadays enchanting the tip in putting into practice and constructing worth by means of artificial brainpower across all solicitations and diligences.

The skillful application of AI may help China to catch up and surpass the United States. According to Lee, this will also support folk's re-experience what it means to be humanoid. He believes that the whole job market will drastically change. You will be using more of AI human brainpower. These are precise AI engines that explain communal hitches at a stretch. For example, drivers that can make loan decisions foe banks, or robotics which can perform chores like washing dishes or fruit picking. Although this could mean some human jobs will be replaced, AI will be good at producing tools for creative and professionals.

Factors Helping China to Become an AI Superpower Quickly

The Chinese government is determined to lead the world in artificial intelligence by the year 2030. Experts tend to agree with China's ambitious goals. It is expected that by 2020, China would have caught up with the united states in AI. Experts also believe that if they maintain their trajectory, China would be far ahead of the United States by the year 2025, and by the year 2030, China will be dominating the industries of AI.

With a GDP of $14 trillion, China is projected to a justification for above 35% of the ecosphere's commercial progress from 2017-2019. This is almost double the United States' GDP prediction of 18%. China's impressive growth is credited to its use of AI across the major industries.

PricewaterhouseCoopers has projected that AI's deployment in strategic industries swill help adds an additional $15 trillion to the international GDP using China captivating a big chunk of that at $7 trillion. North America is expected to take home a paltry $3.7 trillion in expansions. In 2017, China accounted for

48% of the biosphere's overall start-up backing as equated to the united states' 38%.

By this time, the Chinese money in AI imperfections and self-directed automobiles have extended $300 billion, with Chinese companies like Alibaba pledging to invest a lot of resources in international research labs in the United States and Israel.

According to Kai-Fu, there are four main factors which have helped China to move very fast to the top list of the world AI superpowers:

Availability of Data

China is taking advantage of its significant quantity of data to make great leaps in Artificial intelligence. China's Tencent WeChat stage without help has above one billion on the go recurrent consumers. This surpasses the combined population of Europe. When it comes to mobile spending, China beats the United States by a proportion of 50:1. Furthermore, Chinese disbursements on e-commerce are just about double that of the united states.

China is also witnessing an explosion of online to offline startup us, which are helping in making more data available. Another key advantage of Chinese Data is that they concentrate all their data in one place. Chinese AI businesses like Tencent have generated a combined operational network, while Americas' data tends to be spread across various platforms. A key example is American overpayment and transportation data, which are fragmented across multiple platforms.

If you compare mobile payment data between the two countries, you get exciting facts. While the United States saw $112 billion substance of portable disbursements in 2016, Chinese portable disbursements situated over 49 trillion in the similar time. This means AI developers can mine crucial data from Chinese mobile payments like WeChat Wallet and Alipay.

This permits them to produce maps monitoring hundreds of millions of operators every single interchange.

With the upswing of bike-sharing startups like Chinas' ofo and Mobike, Chinese syndicates can construct the use of profoundly surfaced maps of inhabitants association. This permits them to understand the whole thing from your operational practices to your spending mundane.

And as the Chinese's AI facemask acknowledgment aptitudes progress, the maps are gradually being uninhabited with appearances whether you are available or disconnected.

Chinese AI syndicates are assimilated operators' online performances with their bodily biosphere. And as they do so, the Data they collect gives them a significant advantage over their competitors in the United States.

AI Expertise

Although China is still new to the United States in artificial intelligence, china's AI researcher has caught up with the states. When deep learning in the United States made a successful breakthrough in 2012, China was in its initial stages in the AI revolution.

But while AI researchers are still located mainly in the United States, be in support of something businesses like Google, Chinese tech enterprises are rapidly concluding in. At this time, in Academia, Chinese Artificial brainpower scholars are at the same level as those of the united states. For example, an equivalent sum of conventional papers originated from the nations and China in the recent 2017 AAAI conference.

There also has been a noted increase in the partnership amongst china's top tech corporations and developing undergraduate flair. For example, tech firm Tencent has been sponsoring students at an AI lab in Hong Kong's school of science and expertise. The students are also granted access to billions of WeChat data. Moreover, leading Chinese tech firms like Baidu, Didi, and Tencent have all established their specific investigation firms.

As a result of these investments, AI Chinese companies are now leading the world in some technologies. For example, china's appearance++ these days tops the biosphere in appearance and duplicate acknowledgment AI. They beat American companies like Google and Microsoft and Facebook in the 2017 COCO appearance acknowledgment antagonism.

Chinese's speech acknowledgment corporation iFlyTek has outcompeted America voice recognition companies such as Alphabet's DeepMind, Facebook, and IBM Watson in likely linguistic dispensation.

China's Aggressive Entrepreneurs

China's impersonator age saw a big movement of shoddy goods and fake impression. However, this ear helped to inaugurate approximately the utmost inexpensive and hostile industrialists in the biosphere. In fact, China is into inconceivable tough work. Corporations work 9 am to 9 pm. six to seven spells a week shorn of exclusion. Businesspersons are also hard top-down with a solo individual creating all pronouncements. So, the choices are swift. It is all about moving on and executing.

These Chinese tech entrepreneurs have been aggressive in their pursuit to beat the competition. They have devoted a lot of their time and resources to outpace and outsmart parallel startups from elsewhere in the world. It has been noted that the swiftness of the work is abundant quicker in China than in any additional portion of the tech world, like in Silicon Valley. Business opportunities in China are snapped at very fast as compared to the time it takes for tech opportunities to be identified and considered in the United States.

Today, china's AI proficiency has derived from time and startups partake educated to tailor-make American impersonator merchandise to garb the Chinese consumer necessities. These businesspersons are succeeding in getting rid of the copycat tags and are building businesses with no analogs in the United States and Europe.

China has also produced the world's leading AI companies like Baidu, Alibaba, and Tencent. It is also making a significant contribution to the establishment of the world's most valuable AI start upon, such as the Chinese computer startup SenseTime. The startup is currently the most valuable AI start-up in the world. The AI startup product has features that make it possible for your face to be identified as well as your age. It can also determine your impending procuring routines. SenseTime is, nowadays, foremost the biosphere in face pack appreciation machinery smearing their AI to the whole thing from transportation investigation to worker endorsement.

China is also home to over 160 unicorns valued at over $600 billion. China is using its growing expertise to advance further their AI startup agenda.

China's Favorable Government Policies

The Chinese government has issued plans to mark China as the worldwide epicenter of AI modernization with the aim of 1 trillion RMB AI industry by the year 2020. This is an equivalent of $ 150 billion USD.

After the announcement of these grand plans, the Chinese VC investors have invested huge sums into AI startups. Besides, the chines government has been spending a lot of money on their STEM research, which has seen it grow by double digits in recent years.

Besides, China's political system has engaged in recreation, a vital character in the progression of AI research. Native bureaucrats are incentivized to outcompete others in CPP advantages. Because of this arrangement, each leader is striving to win over AI businesses and businesspersons with substantial subventions and satisfactory guidelines.

Mayors transversely the nation have assembled out modernism zone, incubators, and government-backed VC monies. All are unfluctuating paying for expenses of researchers such as rent. This has played a favorable environment for AI startups

Moreover, China is set to capitalize $2 billion in AI expansion park. The park will stock up to 400 AI initiatives and a nationwide AI lab, copyrights, communal invention, and a driving R&D. Besides, the province of Hangzhou has also propelled its personal AI park with a deposit of $1.6 billion USD. There are other cities and regions totaling 19, which are investing a lot of resources on AI is driven city infrastructure as well as on policy development.

Cities like Xiongan Innovative Zone are constructing all-inclusive AI cities in the succeeding two periods. The cities majorly focus on the development of self-directed automobiles, solar panel entrenched infrastructures, and CPU vision geared set-up.

In addition, China's local governments are collaborating with the country's prominent AI tech corporations to derive up with business facilities. As an outcome, corporations like Baidu, Alibaba, Tencent, and iFlyTek are accompanying with countrywide administrations like China's National Engineering Lab for Subterranean Scholarship Skills to invent AI research.

The government has also made available funds for ai innovation and development. The Chinese startups and established tech firms are making use of these funds to grow further and develop new AI products. China's lead in AI appears well established with the help of lavishness of straightforwardly reachable administration funds, smooth infrastructural refurbishments, prominent AI inquiries, and aggressive entrepreneurs base.

As a result of all these factors, the usage of AI in China is no slower enigmatic. AI is no further extensive views as very advanced technology that few enjoy. AI is a nowadays vulnerable cradle, and new alumni from the institution are expected to start using AI engineering to build AI products in a few years to come.

China's New AI Superpower Status, Its Implications, And the New Order

Subsequently closely four eras as the industrial unit of the biosphere, China nowadays is treading into the unique characters in the worldwide budget. The country is considered the leading pivot for pioneering submissions of artificial brainpower. Conferring to one current tale, by PricewaterhouseCoopers, of the $15.7 trillion in international treasure AI is anticipated to breed by the year 2030, China is expected to contribute $7 trillion alone.

It is expected that in the coming days, China's world-class entrepreneurs will apply deep learning to any problem that promises huge profits across all the industries. They are being aided by Silicon Valley's weakness at unwillingness and resistance to localization. As compared to the earlier internet services, AI has a much higher localization quotient. As a result, every divergence between Chinese preference and the standard global product will become an opening which local competitors will attack.

Social Implications

The rise of China as the world's AI superpower could come with several implications. There can occur a large-scale communal complaint and politically aware downfall initiated by pervasive joblessness and wide-open difference. In the coming days, AI will have great potential to disrupt and destroy lives with the expected impact on labor markets and social systems.

The emerging platforms leveraging an AI foundation have a natural affinity for a winner take all economics eroding the competitive mechanisms of markets in the process. This is likely to occur across all industries with a skill bias that divides the job market and squeezes out the middle class.

Economic Implications

Moreover, inequality is expected to rise as a higher meditation of capital gets in the influences of a few. The gap amongst the rich and the unfortunate will remain to grow at an individual level as well as at country levels. As the robot operated factories continue to move closer to the markets, the ladder which the developing countries use to climb out of Poverty will be cut off.

There will be a widespread struggle because people take part been trained to develop a sagacity of value from functioning. The intensification of AI will encounter these standards and intimidate them into weakening this logic of lifetime tenacity.

Implications of Jobs

The rise of AI will definitely have a negative impact on jobs. Within 15 years, AI is estimated to be capable of eliminating over 50% of US jobs as a result of one to one replacement and ground-up disruptions.

In addition, existing high paying professions like medicine will take a different path to the same end. As intelligent machines surpass human's ability to diagnose diseases and recommend treatments, the doctor's role will be significantly limited.

Implications of AI on Global Peace

Military planners both in America and China conquer that AI makes war more likely. Autonomous systems may create a conflict waged by robots less costly in terms of human casualties, but the systems also make conflict more likely because AI will be deciding the speed and the course of the war. China's military and political leaders believe that by 2025, autonomous weapons will run the battlefield with minimal human engagement. It is very easy to see why such prospects could easily destabilize the fragile world peace.

Conclusion

Thank you for making it through to the end of *Artificial Intelligence for Beginners: Easy to Understand Guide of AI, Data Science, and Internet of Things. How to Use AI in Practice? Revelations of AI Superpowers Explained for the Real World.* Let's hope that it was informational and was able to provide you with the basic knowledge you need to understand the concepts of Artificial Intelligence and related technology. By finishing this book, you will be able to possess the mastery that you seek in understanding the role of artificial intelligence in influencing human behaviors, and its impact on the career market.

We have gone through the definition, goals, and types of artificial intelligence and its relationship with emerging technologies, including robotics and the Internet of Things (IoT). This book has offered easy-to-use but very powerful and effective definition of concepts that are crucial in understanding artificial intelligence. It provides a great overview of how the world is gradually adapting to technological changes with the aid of artificial intelligence. You are now familiar with the relationship between AI and robotics and IoT, as well as the possible differences. You have also learned that almost every aspect of our careers is gradually embracing AI for efficiency.

Having understood the key concepts of AI, its goals, and how it works, the next thing you would want to do is to decide to invest in the field due to the vast opportunities available. Currently, China is at the top in the investment on AI-related technology with mega giants such as Google and Amazon following suit. With the knowledge provided in the book, you can learn the more opportunities that exist in such technology.

Finally, if you found this book useful in any way, a review on Amazon is always appreciated!

www.ingramcontent.com/pod-product-compliance
Lightning Source LLC
Chambersburg PA
CBHW071550080326
40690CB00056B/1623